# THE TAO OF
# WALT WHITMAN

# THE TAO OF WALT WHITMAN

## DAILY INSIGHTS AND ACTIONS
## TO ACHIEVE A BALANCED LIFE

CONNIE SHAW and IKE ALLEN

First Sentient Publications edition 2011
Copyright © 2011 by Connie Shaw and Ike Allen

A paperback original

Cover design by Kim Johansen, Black Dog Design
Book design by Kim Johansen, Black Dog Design

Library of Congress Cataloging-in-Publication Data

Shaw, Connie, 1948-
  The Tao of Walt Whitman : daily insights and actions to achieve a balanced life / Connie Shaw and Ike Allen. — 1st Sentient Publications ed.
     p. cm.
  ISBN 978-1-59181-104-6
  1. Conduct of life. 2. Philosophical counseling. 3. Whitman, Walt, 1819-1892—Philosophy. 4. Wisdom in literature. 5. Taoist philosophy. I. Allen, Ike, 1969- II. Title.
  BJ1595.S445 2010
  811'.3—dc22

                           2010039485


Printed in the United States of America

10 9 8 7 6 5 4 3 2 1

SENTIENT PUBLICATIONS
A Limited Liability Company
1113 Spruce Street
Boulder, CO 80302
www.sentientpublications.com

# CONTENTS

# INTRODUCTION

WALT WHITMAN was one of the greatest poets of the twentieth century, whose mysticism, lyricism, and great heart has made him beloved by many. He is the poet of the people: "The messages of great poets to each man and woman are, Come to us on equal terms, Only then can you understand us, We are no better than you, What we enclose you enclose, What we enjoy you may enjoy." And he was—we would like to profess—Taoist in spirit, whether he called himself that or not.

We aren't Whitman scholars, but we know a good poet when we read one. And Whitman has all the elements we love: gorgeous language, a fearless ability to dive into the center of mystery, and an all-embracing attitude toward life. Neither are we Taoist masters—rather, pilgrims on the bumpy path of insight who appreciate a hardy fellow traveler like our poet. Here's how he describes himself: "Walt Whitman, an American, one of the roughs, a kosmos, disorderly, fleshly, and sensual, no sentimentalist, no stander above men or women or apart from them, no more modest than immodest." He was a man exhilarated by the sublime beauty of nature, who celebrated eternity in the everyday—and this is why we call him Taoist.

Taoism is the ancient Chinese philosophical and spiritual tradition that emphasizes compassion, humility, and moderation. (Whitman had the first two in abundance; but the third, one could argue, was not his forte.) Tao is the energy of life, and so it encompasses both the practical and the mystical. The key is to find the balance between them, and this is our objective in *The Tao of Walt Whitman*.

Says the literary critic Harold Bloom, "If you are American, then Walt Whitman is your imaginative father and mother, even if, like myself, you have never composed a line of verse. You can nominate a fair number of literary works as candidates for the secular Scripture of the United States. They might include Melville's *Moby-Dick*, Twain's *Adventures of Huckleberry Finn*, and Emerson's two series of Essays and *The Conduct of Life*. None of those, not even Emerson's, are as central as the first edition of *Leaves of Grass*."

So in this volume we have applied the Whitman scriptures to daily life, to Tao. We've chosen a Taoist principle for each week of the year, and a Whitman verse that expresses or comments on that principle for each day, Monday through Saturday. We've given you something to do or reflect on for the day with the aim of plumbing the depths of Taoist Whitman wisdom and fully experiencing the beauty and truth therein. On Sundays we offer our own experience of, or reflection on, the weekly adventures.

Please use this book in any way that is useful to you. It isn't meant to be a taskmaster. Don't feel as though you must proceed in a linear fashion if that is not your wont. Poetry, and Taoism, and most certainly Whitman, are agents of freedom above all. He was certainly one to shake things up; it is our hope that you will question the need for anything stale and no longer vital in your life as you contemplate his words and take these actions.

You can switch the actions around to suit your schedule, the seasons, or your whims. Sunday is a day to reflect on the week's passages and actions. If you haven't completed them, however, you can take the time to do so on Sunday. You can also go to *dailytao.net* to write about your own experience of the week and read what others have to say.

Feel free to extend any action, insight, or inspiration for another day, week, month…or the rest of your life. Whatever you do, we hope you enjoy, and find inspiration and benefit from the words of this great American poet.

The words of the true poems give you more than poems,
They give you to form for yourself poems, religions, politics, war,
peace, behavior, histories, essays, daily life, and every thing else

## WEEK 1

# TRUTH

## MONDAY

All truths wait in all things,

They neither hasten their own delivery nor resist it,

They do not need the obstetric forceps of the surgeon,

The insignificant is as big to me as any,

What is less or more than a touch?

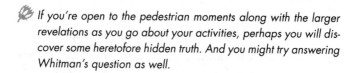 *If you're open to the pedestrian moments along with the larger revelations as you go about your activities, perhaps you will discover some heretofore hidden truth. And you might try answering Whitman's question as well.*

## TUESDAY

Only what proves itself to every man and woman is so

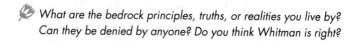 *What are the bedrock principles, truths, or realities you live by? Can they be denied by anyone? Do you think Whitman is right?*

## WEDNESDAY

O truth of the earth! O truth of things! I am determined to
    press the whole way toward you,
Sound your voice! I scale mountains or dive in the sea after
    you.

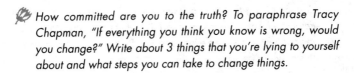 How committed are you to the truth? To paraphrase Tracy
Chapman, "If everything you think you know is wrong, would
you change?" Write about 3 things that you're lying to yourself
about and what steps you can take to change things.

## THURSDAY

The earth does not withhold, it is generous enough,
The truths of the earth continually wait, they are not so
    conceal'd either,
They are calm, subtle, untransmissible by print,
They are imbued through all things conveying themselves
    willingly

Give a try at expressing one of "the truths of the earth" in some
way other than through words. Perhaps paint a picture, dance a
dance, create a melody…

## FRIDAY

All must have reference to the ensemble of the world, and the
   compact truth of the world,
There shall be no subject too pronounced

 *Take one of your most firmly held beliefs and go through your day imagining that the opposite is true. For example, if you sincerely feel that someone in your daily sphere presents a challenge to your wellbeing, take every opportunity to notice ways in which this may not be so.*

## SATURDAY

What do you suppose creation is?
What do you suppose will satisfy the soul, except to walk free
   and own no superior?
What do you suppose I would intimate to you in a hundred
   ways, but that man or woman is as good as God?
And that there is no God any more divine than Yourself?

 *Spend time contemplating the meaning of this. Is this true?*

# SUNDAY

*I spent this week continuously asking myself what I could actually say was true. What was true for me? I noticed that my truth was not necessarily true for others. By the end of the week, I noticed that the only thing it seemed everyone could agree on was that we were all having a common experience. Beyond that, it seemed we each translated truth in our way to support us in this experience. What is true for me is that I create my own truths and I choose to create ideas that make my experience here filled with joy by whatever name. I invite you to enjoy your truths and embrace the truth others share with you. –iKE*

**WEEK 2**

# INFINITE POSSIBILITIES

## MONDAY

See ever so far, there is limitless space outside of that,
Count ever so much, there is limitless time around that.

 *Time is limitless, so take 20 minutes out of infinity to do whatever you most want to do. Take a walk and observe the beauty around you; eat a cupcake; sing a song; give a massage; get a massage...*

## TUESDAY

I know I have the best of time and space, and was never measured and never will be measured.

 *What's the most limiting belief you have about yourself? Take a step to conquer this perceived limitation. If you're afraid of heights, sign up for a skydiving class. If you think you're unattractive, ask someone out on a date...*

## WEDNESDAY

Unseen buds, infinite, hidden well,

Under the snow and ice, under the darkness, in every square or
cubic inch,

Germinal, exquisite, in delicate lace, microscopic, unborn,

Like babes in wombs, latent, folded, compact, sleeping

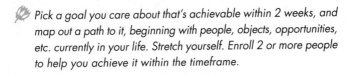 *Sometimes life whispers. The subtlest impulses, if paid attention
to, can result in significant change. Attune yourself to the small
voices that prompt you throughout your day, and discover any
unseen buds that could unfold into something larger.*

## THURSDAY

I do not doubt that whatever can possibly happen anywhere at
any time, is provided for in the inherences of things

*Pick a goal you care about that's achievable within 2 weeks, and
map out a path to it, beginning with people, objects, opportunities,
etc. currently in your life. Stretch yourself. Enroll 2 or more people
to help you achieve it within the timeframe.*

------------------------------------------------------------

# FRIDAY

The boundless vista and the horizon far and dim are all here,
And this is ocean's poem.

 *Think the biggest thought you can manage. Now expand that. Keep it going out to infinity. Now farther. Keep breathing. Write a poem.*

------------------------------------------------------------

# SATURDAY

The soul,

Forever and forever—longer than soil is brown and solid—
longer than water ebbs and flows.

 *What do you think the soul is? Is it the essence? Locate the soul of everything and everyone you meet, and find your relationship to it.*

# SUNDAY

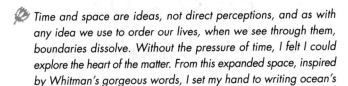

*Time and space are ideas, not direct perceptions, and as with any idea we use to order our lives, when we see through them, boundaries dissolve. Without the pressure of time, I felt I could explore the heart of the matter. From this expanded space, inspired by Whitman's gorgeous words, I set my hand to writing ocean's poem.*

*The sentient sea unfurls
wave upon wave, urgent
over the mirrored sand
—Connie*

## WEEK 3

# PARADOX

## MONDAY

Do I contradict myself?
Very well then I contradict myself,
I am large, I contain multitudes.

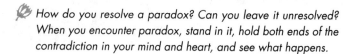 *How do you resolve a paradox? Can you leave it unresolved? When you encounter paradox, stand in it, hold both ends of the contradiction in your mind and heart, and see what happens.*

## TUESDAY

Clear and sweet is my soul, and clear and sweet is all that is
not my soul.

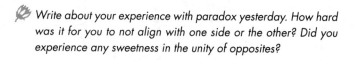 *Write about your experience with paradox yesterday. How hard was it for you to not align with one side or the other? Did you experience any sweetness in the unity of opposites?*

# WEDNESDAY

The eternal equilibrium of things is great, and the eternal
    overthrow of things is great,
And there is another paradox.

*Can you have creation without destruction? Life without death?
Try to imagine this.*

# THURSDAY

Great is Wickedness—I find I often admire it, just as much as
    I admire goodness.
Do you call that a paradox? It certainly is a paradox.

*Play a wickedly fun, creative, loving joke on one of your dearest
friends – make him or her fall over laughing.*

## FRIDAY

Great is Life, real and mystical, wherever and whoever,
Great is Death—sure as Life holds all parts together, Death
    holds all parts together.
Sure as the stars return again after they merge in the light,
    death is great as life.

 *Do something that shows your appreciation for someone currently significant in your life and someone who has passed away.*

## SATURDAY

Great is Youth—equally great is Old Age—great are the Day
    and Night;
Great is Wealth—great is Poverty—great is
Expression—great is Silence.

 *Give someone money and ask someone for money. How do you feel in each situation? Why?*

# SUNDAY

Tao invariably takes no action,

And yet there is nothing left undone.

—Tao Te Ching, in Chan 1963, 158

*What is a paradox? Does it exist in reality or in your mind? Think about what you learned this week and how you can expand that insight into areas of your life that feel stuck.*

*This week, I experienced countless situations that could clearly be seen as "good" or "bad." I remembered it was my judgment that made everything what it was. Am I God or am I iKE? It gave me the opportunity to constantly practice one of the tools I teach in workshops...thinking in terms of **and** instead of **or**. For instance, "It's snowing today, so I can't ride my bike and now I can stay inside and read poetry by the fire. **And** removes the urge to live deeply in the separation by embracing both ends of duality. –iKE*

## WEEK 4

# ACCEPTANCE

## MONDAY

I feel in myself that I represent falsehoods equally with the rest,
And that the universe does.

 *Suspend your judgments. Put aside likes and dislikes, true and false, and just for today, welcome everything that comes your way in a spirit of acceptance, without making distinctions about it. (Note that acceptance doesn't dictate a particular behavior in response.)*

## TUESDAY

Welcome is every organ and attribute of me, and of any man
    hearty and clean,
Not an inch nor a particle of an inch is vile, and none shall be
    less familiar than the rest.

 *Stand in front of the mirror naked for 15 minutes and observe your reactions to what you see.*

# WEDNESDAY

Only what nobody denies is so.

*Do you think this is true? Why or why not? Find someone to discuss this idea with, or write about it.*

# THURSDAY

Not you alone proud truths of the world,
Nor you alone ye facts of modern science,
But myths and fables of eld, Asia's, Africa's fables,
The far-darting beams of the spirit, the unloos'd dreams,
The deep diving bibles and legends

*If you're practical, logical, and left-brained, get in touch with your "far-darting beams of the spirit" by finding evidence in a book or on the Internet that scientists can be mystics. Likewise, if you're the creative, right-brained type, explore science's attempts to understand consciousness and creativity.*

# FRIDAY

...the truth includes all, and is compact just as
 much as space is compact,
And henceforth I will go celebrate any thing I see or am,
And sing and laugh and deny nothing.

*Meet everyone with the realization that you are looking at yourself.*

# SATURDAY

...there is no flaw or vacuum in the amount of
the truth—but...all is truth without exception

*Sometimes life is trying to tell you something through avenues that at first don't look promising. Be alert to the message that an unwelcome experience may have for you.*

# SUNDAY

The great Tao flows everywhere.
It may go left or right.

—Chuang-tzu, in Chan 1963, 186

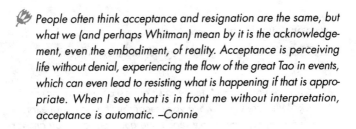 *People often think acceptance and resignation are the same, but what we (and perhaps Whitman) mean by it is the acknowledgement, even the embodiment, of reality. Acceptance is perceiving life without denial, experiencing the flow of the great Tao in events, which can even lead to resisting what is happening if that is appropriate. When I see what is in front me without interpretation, acceptance is automatic. —Connie*

## WEEK 5

# INQUIRY

## MONDAY

I see your rounded never-erased flow,

I see 'neath the rims of your haggard and mean disguises.

*Who are you? Ask someone to sit opposite you and repeatedly ask "Who are you?" while you respond with words that express your identity. They simply repeat the question, and you answer it, until no further dialog is possible.*

## TUESDAY

I myself but write one or two indicative words for the future,

I but advance a moment only to wheel and hurry back in the darkness.

*List 10 traits you have—5 that you think of as positive and 5 negative. Then, one by one, consider how each "positive" trait could be viewed as having negative attributes, and vice versa.*

## WEDNESDAY

I understand your anguish, but I cannot help you,
I approach, hear, behold, the sad mouth, the look out of the
eyes, your mute inquiry

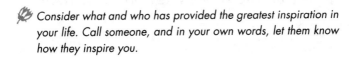 Go outside for a walk alone and ask yourself, "What would my life look like if it was in perfect balance?" Now, take one action to achieve more balance.

## THURSDAY

Never were such sharp questions ask'd as this day,
Never was average man, his soul, more energetic, more like a
God

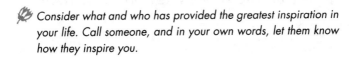 Consider what and who has provided the greatest inspiration in your life. Call someone, and in your own words, let them know how they inspire you.

## FRIDAY

The efflux of the soul comes from within through embower'd
    gates, ever provoking questions,
These yearnings why are they? these thoughts in the darkness
    why are they?

*Think of the 3 people closest to you in your life. Ask yourself, why them?*

## SATURDAY

Not words of routine this song of mine,
But abruptly to question, to leap beyond yet nearer bring

*What could you do to refresh your creativity and energy? Go do it!*

## SUNDAY

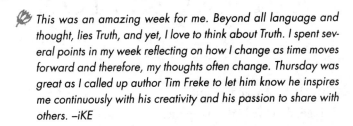 *This was an amazing week for me. Beyond all language and thought, lies Truth, and yet, I love to think about Truth. I spent several points in my week reflecting on how I change as time moves forward and therefore, my thoughts often change. Thursday was great as I called up author Tim Freke to let him know he inspires me continuously with his creativity and his passion to share with others. –iKE*

# APPRECIATION

## MONDAY

Great is To-day, and beautiful,
It is good to live in this age—there never was any better.

 *Do you appreciate simply being in this place, in this time?*

## TUESDAY

Dead poets, philosophs, priests,
Martyrs, artists, inventors, governments long since,
Language-shapers on other shores,
Nations once powerful, now reduced, withdrawn, or desolate,
I dare not proceed till I respectfully credit what you have left
    wafted hither,
I have perused it, own it is admirable, (moving awhile among it)

 *Call, email or Facebook a friend this morning and let them know you are thinking about them.*

# WEDNESDAY

For gentle words, caresses, gifts from foreign lands,
For shelter, wine and meat—for sweet appreciation,
(You distant, dim unknown—or young or old—countless,
   unspecified, readers belov'd,
We never met, and neer shall meet—and yet our souls
   embrace, long, close and long;)

 *Express to someone you've never met how they've influenced your
life. Perhaps it's a politician, spiritual leader, musician... Write
them a letter or email and send it if you have their address.*

# THURSDAY

I hear the sound I love, the sound of the human voice,
I hear all sounds running together, combined, fused or
   following,
Sounds of the city and sounds out of the city, sounds of the
   day and night

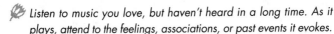 *Listen to music you love, but haven't heard in a long time. As it
plays, attend to the feelings, associations, or past events it evokes.*

## FRIDAY

I bequeath myself to the dirt to grow from the grass I love,
If you want me again look for me under your boot-soles.

 Who has come and gone in your life that made a difference for you? Find a way to remember them and acknowledge what they gave you.

## SATURDAY

…all beautiful to me, all wondrous,
My limbs and the quivering fire that ever plays through them,
    for reasons, most wondrous,
Existing I peer and penetrate still,
Content with the present, content with the past

 Spend 30 minutes in a space you enjoy and be still. Perhaps it's your living room or a park bench. Consider all that is provided to you without any effort on your part.

# SUNDAY

*Ultimately, nothing is my doing, and yet I have access to everything. This seems to me like magic! All I need do is engage what comes my way with full heart, mind, and soul—and listen to Nada Surf. –Connie*

**WEEK 7**

# AUTHENTICITY

## MONDAY

Stop this day and night with me and you shall possess the
origin of all poems,

You shall possess the good of the earth and sun, (there are
millions of suns left,)

You shall no longer take things at second or third hand, nor
look through the eyes of the dead, nor feed on the spectres
in books,

You shall not look through my eyes either, nor take things
from me,

You shall listen to all sides and filter them from your self.

 *Pretend for a moment that you've never read a single self-help,
spiritual, or inspirational book, and write a page or two of your
own rock-bottom truths, completely in your own words.*

# TUESDAY

One's-self must never give way—that is the final substance—
    that out of all is sure,
Out of politics, triumphs, battles, life, what at last finally
    remains?
When shows break up what but One's-Self is sure?

 *What do you know about yourself that events in your life can never change?*

# WEDNESDAY

Think nothing can ever be greater, nothing can ever deserve
    more than it deserves,
Regarding it all intently a long while, then dismissing it,
I stand in my place with my own day here.

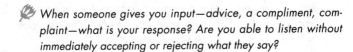 *When someone gives you input—advice, a compliment, complaint—what is your response? Are you able to listen without immediately accepting or rejecting what they say?*

# THURSDAY

The true words do not fail, for motion does not fail and
    reflection does not fail,
Also the day and night do not fail, and the voyage we pursue
    does not fail.

 *Write about a current goal and the obstacles that may be placed in your path. Come up with strategies for overcoming those obstacles.*

# FRIDAY

Each man to himself and each woman to herself, is the word
    of the past and present, and the true word of immortality;
No one can acquire for another—not one,
Not one can grow for another—not one.

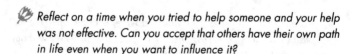 *Reflect on a time when you tried to help someone and your help was not effective. Can you accept that others have their own path in life even when you want to influence it?*

## SATURDAY

Your true soul and body appear before me,

They stand forth out of affairs, out of commerce, shops, work,
   farms, clothes, the house, buying, selling, eating, drinking,
   suffering, dying.

*For this one day, put aside your busy illusions and simply experience the current of life—your true soul and body.*

## SUNDAY

*Friday's lesson! I've spent much of my life in an attempt to help others, even when they didn't truly want my help or their path was not one in which they could receive my assistance. I've noticed this tendency this week. I am authentically hard wired to help others...I guess that is part of my own life path. –iKE*

**WEEK 8**

# SILENCE

## MONDAY

I think I will do nothing for a long time but listen
And accrue what I hear into myself....and let sounds
    contribute toward me.

 *Try responding as concisely as possible to the things people say to you. Put your attention on listening, rather than speech.*

## TUESDAY

I swear I see what is better than to tell the best,
It is always to leave the best untold.

 *Use as many nonverbal modes of expression as you have at your command. Consider communicating via facial expressions, gifts, your choice of clothing. Have fun!*

# WEDNESDAY

I swear I begin to see little or nothing in audible words,

All merges toward the presentation of the unspoken meanings
of the earth,

Toward him who sings the songs of the body and of the truths
of the earth,

Toward him who makes the dictionaries of words that print
cannot touch.

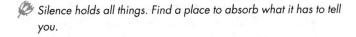 *Instead of **saying** kind things to people, **do** kind things. Open a door for someone, smile, do a favor...*

# THURSDAY

What do you seek so pensive and silent?

*Silence holds all things. Find a place to absorb what it has to tell you.*

# FRIDAY

Writing and talk do not prove me,
I carry the plenum of proof and every thing else in my face,
With the hush of my lips I wholly confound the skeptic.

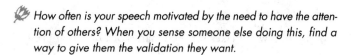 *How often is your speech motivated by the need to have the attention of others? When you sense someone else doing this, find a way to give them the validation they want.*

# SATURDAY

When the subtle air, the impalpable, the sense that words and
    reason hold not, surround us and pervade us,
Then I am charged with untold and untellable wisdom, I am
    silent, I require nothing further

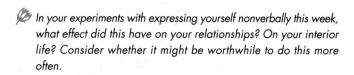 *In your experiments with expressing yourself nonverbally this week, what effect did this have on your relationships? On your interior life? Consider whether it might be worthwhile to do this more often.*

# SUNDAY

*In silence is fullness and mystery. The wild unknown, and the language of the heart. It is where we go when words can no longer express what we need to say, and from it may come our most honest communication. —Connie*

WEEK 9

# COMPASSION

## MONDAY

Whoever degrades another degrades me,
And whatever is done or said returns at last to me.

*Cut out all speech that refers to someone not present, whether what you would have said is something you'd consider to be positive, negative, or neutral. Observe how often this renders you silent.*

## TUESDAY

O the joy of that vast elemental sympathy which only the
human soul is capable of generating and emitting in steady
and limitless floods.

*Make your speech about others only positive in nature. If someone complains to you about another, respond with praise for that person.*

# WEDNESDAY

You convicts in prison-cells, you sentenced assassins chain'd
    and handcuff'd with iron,
Who am I too that I am not on trial or in prison?
Me ruthless and devilish as any, that my wrists are not chain'd
    with iron, or my ankles with iron?

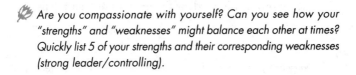

*Have you ever done anything similar to what you've judged
another for? Pick someone you've judged and find a way to
express forgiveness to them.*

# THURSDAY

I announce the great individual, fluid as Nature, chaste,
    affectionate, compassionate, fully arm'd.

*Are you compassionate with yourself? Can you see how your
"strengths" and "weaknesses" might balance each other at times?
Quickly list 5 of your strengths and their corresponding weaknesses
(strong leader/controlling).*

# FRIDAY

My spirit has pass'd in compassion and determination around
the whole earth,
I have look'd for equals and lovers and found them ready for
me in all lands,
I think some divine rapport has equalized me with them.

 *Donate some money to a cause you care about.*

# SATURDAY

Lusts and wickedness are acceptable to me,
I walk with delinquents with passionate love,
I feel I am of them—I belong to those convicts and prostitutes
myself,
And henceforth I will not deny them—for how can I deny
myself?

 *What are you ashamed of in yourself that you then project onto
others? Notice the negative opinions you have of others and reflect
on their origin in your own self-image.*

# SUNDAY

*This week turned out to be a week of receiving countless personal rewards. As I practiced forgiveness, donated my change at every coffee shop, grocery store, etc. I noticed that I did it without judging it positive or negative, and in that space I felt a natural, flowing sense of peace. I've thought much about how everyone is dealt a hand and people are doing the best they can with it. From here, I feel balanced and inspired to support myself and others in their journey. –iKE*

## WEEK 10

# WILDNESS

## MONDAY

Unscrew the locks from the doors!
Unscrew the doors themselves from their jambs!

 *Do something you've never done before, but don't blame us for the consequences!*

## TUESDAY

O the joy of the strong-brawn'd fighter, towering in the arena
    in perfect condition, conscious of power, thirsting to meet
    his opponent.

 *Are you in touch with your aggression? Where is it located in your body? Channel it into something creative.*

## WEDNESDAY

Hark, some wild trumpeter, some strange musician,
Hovering unseen in air, vibrates capricious tunes to-night.
I hear thee trumpeter, listening alert I catch thy notes,
Now pouring, whirling like a tempest round me

 *Dance to your wildest music, either alone or with another.*

## THURSDAY

O to struggle against great odds, to meet enemies undaunted!
To be entirely alone with them, to find how much one can
    stand!
To look strife, torture, prison, popular odium, face to face!
To mount the scaffold, to advance to the muzzles of guns with
    perfect nonchalance!
To be indeed a God!

 *Tune into your divinity—how does it express itself?*

## FRIDAY

O something ecstatic and undemonstrable! O music wild!

 *What's the most fun you can imagine?*

## SATURDAY

O something pernicious and dread!
Something far away from a puny and pious life!
Something unproved! something in a trance!
Something escaped from the anchorage and driving free.

 *Get in the car, drive without knowing what the destination is, and relax!*

# SUNDAY

*I'm guilty of taking myself too seriously. Tapping into wildness unhinges that tendency and provides surprise and revelation. It's often not comfortable, but always alive. –Connie*

## WEEK 11

# MIRACLES

## MONDAY

I believe in the flesh and the appetites,
Seeing, hearing, feeling, are miracles, and each part and tag of
  me is a miracle.

*We take our bodies for granted, but they are exquisite pieces of
machinery. Do something to honor the miracle of your body—get
a massage or a manicure, eat an entirely healthy meal, exercise...*

## TUESDAY

And I will thread a thread through my poems that time and
  events are compact,
And that all the things of the universe are perfect miracles,
  each as profound as any.

*Write something from this perspective.*

## WEDNESDAY

O for the voices of animals—O for the swiftness and balance
of fishes!
O for the dropping of raindrops in a song!
O for the sunshine and motion of waves in a song!

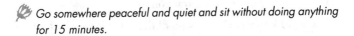 *Each leaf, insect, and blade of grass is an amazing work of art. Go somewhere in nature, even if it's only your back yard, and take a close look at the marvels around you.*

## THURSDAY

What beauty is this that descends upon me and rises out of me?

*Go somewhere peaceful and quiet and sit without doing anything for 15 minutes.*

# FRIDAY

O to realize space!
The plenteousness of all, that there are no bounds,
To emerge and be of the sky, of the sun and moon and flying
clouds, as one with them.

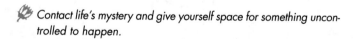 *Sit in a quiet indoor space with your eyes closed. In your mind's eye, feel the center of your body. Now feel the outlines of your body, then the space in the room, then the outlines of the building, the town, the state, the country, the planet. Move your consciousness as far out as it will go, then slowly come back into yourself.*

# SATURDAY

O to attract by more than attraction!
How it is I know not—yet behold! the something which obeys
none of the rest,
It is offensive, never defensive—yet how magnetic it draws.

*Contact life's mystery and give yourself space for something uncontrolled to happen.*

# SUNDAY

*This was a perfect week for me to reflect on miracles as I have been finishing our movie about A Course in Miracles (ACIM). ACIM looks at a miracle as the opportunity for each of us to choose the Right Mind over the Ego Mind. Focusing on this perspective allowed me to see endless miracles as I noticed the perfection in everything around me. Beyond the judgment of my egoic mind, there was only perfection. —iKE*

# NATURE

## MONDAY

A morning-glory at my window satisfies me more than the
   metaphysics of books.

 *Give flowers to someone. Wildflowers count too. (Please look at
tomorrow's insight/action step to prepare for it.)*

## TUESDAY

To behold the day-break!
The little light fades the immense and diaphanous shadows,
The air tastes good to my palate.

 *Get up at dawn and take a walk. Taste the air.*

## WEDNESDAY

Of the smell of apples and lemons, of the pairing of birds,

Of the wet of woods, of the lapping of waves,

Of the mad pushes of waves upon the land, I them chanting

 *Write a song inspired by your walk yesterday and sing it to some-one or record it.*

## THURSDAY

I do not call the tortoise unworthy because she is not
    something else,

And the jay in the woods never studied the gamut, yet trills
    pretty well to me

And the look of the bay mare shames stillness out of me.

 *Take 15 minutes to really look at something man did not create—a plant, a tree, an animal, a mountain.*

# FRIDAY

Frost-mellow'd berries and Third-month twigs offer'd fresh to
young persons wandering out in the fields when the winter
breaks up

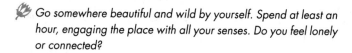 *Take a small child for a walk in the woods, or a park, or the most
untouched place you know. Go at the child's pace. Stop and look
at the flowers when they want to. You're not going anywhere.*

# SATURDAY

I see the plentiful larkspur and wild onions, the barren,
colorless, sage-deserts,
I see in glimpses afar or towering immediately above me the
great mountains

*Go somewhere beautiful and wild by yourself. Spend at least an
hour, engaging the place with all your senses. Do you feel lonely
or connected?*

# SUNDAY

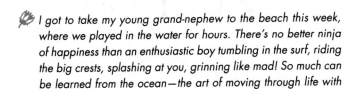 *I got to take my young grand-nephew to the beach this week, where we played in the water for hours. There's no better ninja of happiness than an enthusiastic boy tumbling in the surf, riding the big crests, splashing at you, grinning like mad! So much can be learned from the ocean—the art of moving through life with flexibility, beauty, freedom, power, grace, and joy. —Connie*

# WONDER

## MONDAY

It is no small matter, this round and delicious globe moving so
exactly in its orbit for ever and ever, without one jolt or
the untruth of a single second

 *You can see the perfection of the world if you let it in.*

## TUESDAY

How curious! how real!
Underfoot the divine soil, overhead the sun.

 *Go dig in the dirt...beautify a spot in your yard or repot a house
plant.*

## WEDNESDAY

How they are provided for upon the earth, (appearing at intervals,)
How dear and dreadful they are to the earth,
How they inure to themselves as much as to any—what a
    paradox appears their age,
How people respond to them, yet know them not,
How there is something relentless in their fate all times,
How all times mischoose the objects of their adulation and reward,
And how the same inexorable price must still be paid for the
    same great purchase.

 *What do you think Walt is talking about? What do these words mean to you?*

## THURSDAY

Whoever you are holding me now in hand,
Without one thing all will be useless,
I give you fair warning before you attempt me further,
I am not what you supposed, but far different.

 *What is the one thing without which all will be useless?*

# FRIDAY

I cannot answer the question of appearances or that of identity
    beyond the grave,
But I walk or sit indifferent, I am satisfied

*Do you know what a single thing really is? Do you know what
will happen in the next moment? Does that bother you?*

# SATURDAY

O the engineer's joys! to go with a locomotive!
To hear the hiss of steam, the merry shriek, the steam-whistle,
    the laughing locomotive!
To push with resistless way and speed off in the distance.

*Wonder makes life wonderful, dissolving time and space. Your
life is a complete mystery...enjoy it!*

# SUNDAY

I've noticed that many of the subjects in this book lead me to the same place—one of peace, the unknown, and wonder. Years ago, this state would make me anxious, and now I savor it. Working on this book has led me to stay present to the wonders of the wind, my daughters playing in the yard, a truck passing by—all so delicious and wonder-full. –iKE

## WEEK 14

# ECSTASY

## MONDAY

Exalte, rapt, ecstatic,
The visible but their womb of birth,
Of orbic tendencies to shape and shape and shape,
The mighty earth-eidolon.

*Write a love letter to yourself and mail it. Make it really juicy.*

## TUESDAY

That music always round me, unceasing, unbeginning, yet long
    untaught I did not hear,
But now the chorus I hear and am elated

*Express yourself musically with the fullest ecstatic height of feeling, using instruments and/or voice.*

## WEDNESDAY

It is a painful thing to love a man or woman to excess, and yet
    it satisfies, it is great,
But there is something else very great, it makes the whole
    coincide,
It, magnificent, beyond materials, with continuous hands
    sweeps and provides for all.

 *Write a love letter to God.*

## THURSDAY

Beginning my studies the first step pleas'd me so much,
The mere fact consciousness, these forms, the power of
    motion,
The least insect or animal, the senses, eyesight, love,
The first step I say awed me and pleas'd me so much,
I have hardly gone and hardly wish'd to go any farther,
But stop and loiter all the time to sing it in ecstatic songs.

 *Slow down and pay attention to your body. When you feel any
tension, relax it.*

# FRIDAY

O the horseman's and horsewoman's joys!
The saddle, the gallop, the pressure upon the seat, the cool
   gurgling by the ears and hair.
O the fireman's joys!
I hear the alarm at dead of night,
I hear bells, shouts! I pass the crowd, I run!
The sight of the flames maddens me with pleasure.

 Find the excitement in your life—is it in hiding? Can you coax it
out?

# SATURDAY

O to bathe in the swimming-bath, or in a good place along
   shore,
To splash the water! to walk ankle-deep, or race naked along
   the shore.

 Make water your playground. Soak in the tub, splash in the pool,
or run along the beach.

# SUNDAY

*This was the most difficult week for me so far. To access the full range of ecstasy possible for me, I had to visit some layers of sadness first. –Connie*

# MYSTERY

## MONDAY

Sure as the most certain sure, plumb in the uprights, well
    entretied, braced in the beams,
Stout as a horse, affectionate, haughty, electrical,
I and this mystery here we stand.

*What do you need to do to embrace the mysteries that await you
this week?*

## TUESDAY

Poets to come! orators, singers, musicians to come!
Not to-day is to justify me and answer what I am for,
But you, a new brood, native, athletic, continental, greater than
    before known,
Arouse! for you must justify me.

*Knowing too much can be a liability. Ask someone much younger*

than you for their opinion on something you care about and listen
carefully to what they say without reacting to it.

## WEDNESDAY

I am a man who, sauntering along without fully stopping,

    turns a casual look upon you and then averts his face,

Leaving it to you to prove and define it,

Expecting the main things from you.

*We often assume that we know what others think of us, but do
we really? Try out the attitude that others' opinions of you are
completely unfathomable, unknown, and irrelevant!*

## THURSDAY

Melange mine own, the unseen and the seen,

Mysterious ocean where the streams empty,

Prophetic spirit of materials shifting and flickering around me,

Living beings, identities now doubtless near us in the air that

    we know not of

*We're so fixated on the objects in our world that we don't notice
the space around them. Pay attention to the space around people*

*and things, and observe what happens.*

# FRIDAY

Victory, union, faith, identity, time,

The indissoluble compacts, riches, mystery,

Eternal progress, the kosmos, and the modern reports.

*Don't believe anything you think! (And please look at tomorrow—*
*planning required.)*

# SATURDAY

Let others dispose of questions, I dispose of nothing, I arouse
  unanswerable questions,

Who are they I see and touch, and what about them?

*When you wake up this morning, lie in bed and breathe slowly,*
*calmly, and deeply. Do you feel the mystery? You are everything*
*and nothing. Remember this feeling all weekend.*

# SUNDAY

Life is a continuous mystery. This week, I asked my 5-year-old daughter, Olivia, several questions about life that I have attached judgment to. "Olivia, what do we do if there are 11 people who want to play a game and each team can only have 5 players on it?" Olivia: We could change the rules, 1 person could be the cheerleader or we play a different game that 11 people can play." Never once did she say one person would need to sit out the game. The mystery in my life is ever thinking I "know" how anything really is. –iKE

# TIMELESSNESS

## MONDAY

There was never any more inception than there is now,
Nor any more youth or age than there is now,
And will never be any more perfection than there is now,
Nor any more heaven or hell than there is now.

 *What are you inspired to do? Don't put it off any longer—do it today.*

## TUESDAY

Me imperturbe, standing at ease in Nature,
Master of all or mistress of all, aplomb in the midst of
     irrational things,
Imbued as they, passive, receptive, silent as they,
Finding my occupation, poverty, notoriety, foibles, crimes, less
     important than I thought

🌀 *Go to the wildest place in nature you can find, focus on one thing (tree, flower, rock...), contemplate everything that led to its existence, and consider what may become of it. Birth, death, and renewal. What was the flower before it was a flower? What will it be in its next form?*

## WEDNESDAY

I say no man has ever yet been half devout enough,
None has ever yet adored or worship'd half enough,
None has begun to think how divine he himself is, and how
    certain the future is.

🌀 *Sit in front of a clock and watch the hands move for 5 minutes. Then close your eyes and see if you can actually experience time without a way to measure it. This is a different matter from your thoughts about the past or future.*

## THURSDAY

Not a mark, not a record remains—and yet all remains.

🌀 *Let go of everything that happens. At the end of the day, what do you notice about yourself?*

# FRIDAY

That behind the mask of materials you patiently wait, no
matter how long,
That you will one day perhaps take control of all,
That you will perhaps dissipate this entire show of appearance,
That may-be you are what it is all for, but it does not last so
very long,
But you will last very long.

 *Consider that you may be a divine being expressing itself through your personality. Have you been here before? Would you want to return again? Why?*

# SATURDAY

O the joy of my spirit—it is uncaged—it darts like lightning!
It is not enough to have this globe or a certain time,
I will have thousands of globes and all time.

 *You have all the time in eternity—what will you do with it? Act as though you believe this to be true. (And party like it's 1999 if all else fails.)*

# SUNDAY

*When I let go, I see how much I hold on to. And when I let go of time, I see I can move quickly without hurrying. –Connie*

*If you'd like, visit dailytao.net and let us know how this experiment in poetry and insight is going for you.*

WEEK 17

# ILLUSION

## MONDAY

Ever the mutable,
Ever materials, changing, crumbling, re-cohering,
Ever the ateliers, the factories divine,
Issuing eidolons.

Lo, I or you,
Or woman, man, or state, known or unknown,
We seeming solid wealth, strength, beauty build,
But really build eidolons.

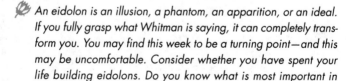

*An eidolon is an illusion, a phantom, an apparition, or an ideal. If you fully grasp what Whitman is saying, it can completely transform you. You may find this week to be a turning point—and this may be uncomfortable. Consider whether you have spent your life building eidolons. Do you know what is most important in your life?*

# TUESDAY

All space, all time,

(The stars, the terrible perturbations of the suns,

Swelling, collapsing, ending, serving their longer, shorter use,)

Fill'd with eidolons only.

*Another wonderful writer said "All the world's a stage, And all the men and women merely players: They have their exits and their entrances; And one man in his time plays many parts." Consider yourself an actor in someone else's script—does that change your perception of how you relate to others, to your own actions?*

# WEDNESDAY

The skies of day and night, colors, densities, forms, may-be these are (as doubtless they are) only apparitions, and the real something has yet to be known

*Now imagine that you're the script writer and have created all the characters in your life (yourself included). Are you enjoying your play? If not, rewrite!*

## THURSDAY

That which eludes this verse and any verse,
Unheard by sharpest ear, unform'd in clearest eye or
     cunningest mind,
Nor lore nor fame, nor happiness nor wealth,
And yet the pulse of every heart and life throughout the world
     incessantly,
Which you and I and all pursuing ever ever miss,
Open but still a secret, the real of the real, an illusion,
Costless, vouchsafed to each, yet never man the owner,
Which poets vainly seek to put in rhyme, historians in prose,
Which sculptor never chisel'd yet, nor painter painted,
Which vocalist never sung, nor orator nor actor ever utter'd,
Invoking here and now I challenge for my song.

 *Create something that expresses "the real of the real." Take Walt up on his challenge.*

## FRIDAY

Have you no thought O dreamer that it may be all maya,
     illusion?

🌀 *What is the other side of that realization? If it's all a dream, what is your response to the dream?*

---

## SATURDAY

See, vast trackless spaces,

As in a dream they change, they swiftly fill

🌀 *"Nature abhors a vacuum" it is said. If this week has cleared some space in the clutter of your life and mind, what will you fill it with?*

---

## SUNDAY

🌀 *This is my favorite week to date as my first movie, Leap!, is all about whether or not our entire reality is an illusion. During the creation of this movie, virtually everything in my life changed. I left my disempowering marriage, went through bankruptcy and faced countless other challenges. It was during this that identifying with my "skin suit" as my primary identity fell away and I experienced the caterpillar to butterfly transition. I now play the role of iKE ALLEN and know that it truly is only a role. –iKE*

## WEEK 18

# DEATH

## MONDAY

Was somebody asking to see the soul?

See, your own shape and countenance, persons, substances,
beasts,

the trees, the running rivers, the rocks and sands.

All hold spiritual joys and afterwards loosen them;

How can the real body ever die and be buried?

 *Who have you lost that you sometimes feel is still near you? Is there something you want to express to them? Communicate whatever that is in some way.*

## TUESDAY

And I will show that there is no imperfection in the present,
and can be none in the future,
And I will show that whatever happens to anybody it may be
turn'd to beautiful results,
And I will show that nothing can happen more beautiful than
death,

*What is the beauty that follows a death of someone you love?
Does it bring you closer to others? Do you appreciate your own
life more?*

## WEDNESDAY

Death is beautiful from you, (what indeed is finally beautiful
except death and love?)

*What does this mean to you? Create something to express it—a
journal entry, a song, a painting...*

# THURSDAY

Life and Death

The two old, simple problems ever intertwined,
Close home, elusive, present, baffled, grappled.
By each successive age insoluble, pass'd on,
To ours to-day—and we pass on the same.

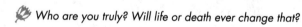 *What was passed on to you by those who came before you?*
*What will you pass on to others when you're gone?*

# FRIDAY

Death or life I am then indifferent, my soul declines to prefer

*Who are you truly? Will life or death ever change that?*

## SATURDAY

Through me shall the words be said to make death
   exhilarating,
Give me your tone therefore O death, that I may accord with it

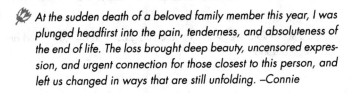 How could death be exhilarating?

## SUNDAY

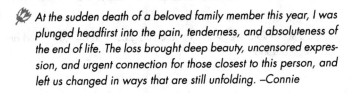 At the sudden death of a beloved family member this year, I was plunged headfirst into the pain, tenderness, and absoluteness of the end of life. The loss brought deep beauty, uncensored expression, and urgent connection for those closest to this person, and left us changed in ways that are still unfolding. —Connie

## WEEK 19

# COMMUNITY

## MONDAY

Fear not O Muse! truly new ways and days receive, surround
   you,
I candidly confess a queer, queer race, of novel fashion,
And yet the same old human race, the same within, without,
Faces and hearts the same, feelings the same, yearnings the same

 *Do some volunteer work in the coming days as an expression of brotherhood.*

## TUESDAY

O the farmer's joys!
…To rise at peep of day and pass forth nimbly to work,
To plough land in the fall for winter-sown crops,
To plough land in the spring for maize,
To train orchards, to graft the trees, to gather apples in the fall.

Who makes it possible for you to have food on your table (farmers, truck drivers, butchers, store clerks...)? What if you had to do all that yourself?! Ponder this...what does it make you think about the food you eat?

## WEDNESDAY

A great city is that which has the greatest men and women,
If it be a few ragged huts it is still the greatest city in the
whole world.

It's the people, not the buildings, that make a community great. Who are 5 people outside of your family (the pharmacist, a teacher, the cop on his beat...) that make the community you're part of wonderful? Acknowledge them in some way.

## THURSDAY

Where the city of the faithfulest friends stands,
Where the city of the cleanliness of the sexes stands,
Where the city of the healthiest fathers stands,
Where the city of the best-bodied mothers stands,
There the great city stands.

*You've just arrived here from Pluto and will be returning home tomorrow. What can you tell your fellow Plutonians about earthlings from observing the community you've visited (your own town or city)?*

## FRIDAY

Who are the infants, some playing, some slumbering?

Who are the girls? who are the married women?

Who are the groups of old men going slowly with their arms about each other's necks?

What do you hear Walt Whitman?

*Go sit on a park bench or someplace else out among people and close your eyes. What do you hear from the people surrounding you? Does it evoke different feelings in you than looking at them does?*

## SATURDAY

Stranger, if you passing meet me and desire to speak to me,

why should you not speak to me?

And why should I not speak to you?

*Strike up a conversation with a stranger.*

## SUNDAY

*What a fun week this was. I spent it interacting with people that I would normally walk by. I also checked in with many friends and family members. In the experience of duality, I have so many amazing people to play with. I borrowed a lawnmower from someone this week, just to see if they would actually share with me and they did. I experienced the anxiety of asking others for help and the joys of seeing that every one of them was willing to do so. Most people seem to want to give and struggle to receive. The majority of us don't like to ask others for help. I invite you to ask for help from others, even if you don't really need it. –iKE*

WEEK 20

# WORK

## MONDAY

The delicious singing of the mother, or of the young wife at
    work, or of the girl sewing or washing,
Each singing what belongs to him or her and to none else

 *What is unique to you in the work that you do today?*

## TUESDAY

The present now and here,
America's busy, teeming, intricate whirl,
Of aggregate and segregate for only thence releasing,
To-day's eidólons.

 *Existence holds nothing and everything in balance. Let stillness
lead to action.*

## WEDNESDAY

Ah little recks the laborer,

How near his work is holding him to God,

The loving Laborer through space and time.

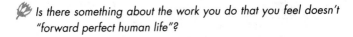

*What do you appreciate about the work you do, whether it is your job, caring for your family, or volunteer efforts? Focus on what is satisfying about this work.*

## THURSDAY

Somewhere within their walls shall all that forwards perfect
   human life be started,

Tried, taught, advanced, visibly exhibited.

Not only all the world of works, trade, products,

But all the workmen of the world here to be represented.

*Is there something about the work you do that you feel doesn't "forward perfect human life"?*

# FRIDAY

To manual work for each and all, to plough, hoe, dig,
To plant and tend the tree, the berry, vegetables, flowers,
For every man to see to it that he really do something, for
    every woman too

 *It can feel wonderful to see the immediate results of your labors. Do something that gives you that satisfaction (plant a rosebush, bake a cake, fix a broken appliance...).*

# SATURDAY

Say on, sayers! sing on, singers!
Delve! mould! pile the words of the earth!
Work on, age after age, nothing is to be lost,
It may have to wait long, but it will certainly come in use,
When the materials are all prepared and ready, the architects
    shall appear.

 *What can you do to make life easier for the architects when they appear?*

# SUNDAY

*I have always loved reading and writing, so I've found a way to do both as my life's work, publishing and writing books. The particular choices I make carry out my purpose, combining the gifts I was given and the influences I've encountered so that I publish this book, not that one, and contribute to the book you hold in your hands. The meaning lies in the uniqueness. –Connie*

## WEEK 21

# GENEROSITY

## MONDAY

Here, take this gift,

I was reserving it for some hero, speaker, or general,

One who should serve the good old cause, the great idea, the
progress and freedom of the race,

Some brave confronter of despots, some daring rebel;

But I see that what I was reserving belongs to you just as much
as to any.

 *Have you been saving up your gifts? Lavish them on everyone
you encounter.*

## TUESDAY

Have I forgotten any part? any thing in the past?

Come to me whoever and whatever, till I give you recognition.

 *Is there someone in your past that you'd like to thank but cannot,*

*perhaps because they have passed on? Give something or do*
*something for someone in your life.*

## WEDNESDAY

The runaway slave came to my house and stopt outside,

I heard his motions crackling the twigs of the woodpile,

Through the swung half-door of the kitchen I saw him limpsy
and weak,

And went where he sat on a log and led him in and assured him,

And brought water and fill'd a tub for his sweated body and
bruis'd feet,

And gave him a room that enter'd from my own, and gave him
some coarse clean clothes,

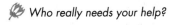 *Who really needs your help?*

## THURSDAY

Of equality—as if it harm'd me, giving others the same
chances and rights as myself—as if it were not indispensable
to my own rights that others possess the same.

Write to a politician, donate to a charity, volunteer for Amnesty International's letter writing program—do something to advance human rights.

# FRIDAY

Sun so generous it shall be you!

 Do something generous that is completely easy and joyful for you to do.

# SATURDAY

I will confront these shows of the day and night,

I will know if I am to be less than they,

I will see if I am not as majestic as they,

I will see if I am not as subtle and real as they,

I will see if I am to be less generous than they,

I will see if I have no meaning, while the houses and ships
have meaning,

I will see if the fishes and birds are to be enough for
themselves, and I am not to be enough for myself.

🍂 Take the most generous action possible towards yourself.

## SUNDAY

🍂 This week caused me to reflect on Community week. In that week, I asked others for assistance frequently. In this week, I offered to help people as much as possible. It was interesting to notice how some people easily allowed me to help them while the majority wanted to do things themselves. It seems as if people in our society are very independent and would possibly enjoy life more if they became a bit more interdependent. –iKE

WEEK 22

# PASSION

## MONDAY

I give nothing as duties,

What others give as duties I give as living impulses,

(Shall I give the heart's action as a duty?)

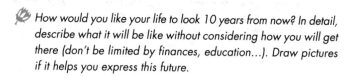 *How would you like your life to look 10 years from now? In detail, describe what it will be like without considering how you will get there (don't be limited by finances, education...). Draw pictures if it helps you express this future.*

## TUESDAY

I will make the songs of passion to give them their way

*It is now 10 years in the future. Your passionate direction for your life has borne fruit. Your future self has some advice for your present self—write it down.*

# WEDNESDAY

Know'st thou the excellent joys of youth?
Joys of the dear companions and of the merry word and
   laughing face?
Joy of the glad light-beaming day, joy of the wide-breath'd
   games?
Joy of sweet music, joy of the lighted ball-room and the dancers?
Joy of the plenteous dinner, strong carouse and drinking?

*Have as much fun as you possibly can today...*

# THURSDAY

I will therefore let flame from me the burning fires that were
   threatening to consume me,
I will lift what has too long kept down those smouldering
   fires,
I will give them complete abandonment

*...just don't get arrested.*

## FRIDAY

These furies, elements, storms, motions of Nature, throes of
    apparent dissolution, you are he or she who is master or
    mistress over them,
Master or mistress in your own right over Nature, elements,
    pain, passion, dissolution.

*Can you see how you might achieve the goals you have for your
life and enjoy the process?*

## SATURDAY

Of Life immense in passion, pulse, and power,
Cheerful, for freest action form'd under the laws divine,
The Modern Man I sing.

*You can be passionate about anything. Bring that spirit to your
entire day.*

# SUNDAY

*I don't tend to do a lot of planning—I'm more likely to jump in and go with something that holds a lot of energy for me than to work by some grand design. Which is not to say I don't have thoughts about how I'd like things to turn out. Writing about a vision for my future gave me a different lens for looking at the way I spend my time now. Passion can lead you anywhere if you are fully committed. —Connie*

# BALANCE

## MONDAY

Omnes! omnes! let others ignore what they may,

I make the poem of evil also, I commemorate that part also,

I am myself just as much evil as good, and my nation is—and I
    say there is in fact no evil,

(Or if there is I say it is just as important to you, to the land or
    to me, as any thing else.)

*The way of Tao is the way of balance. Whitman understood this
profoundly. If there is in fact no ultimate evil (or good) then what
is the rudder for the ship of your life?*

## TUESDAY

I find one side a balance and the antipodal side a balance,

Soft doctrine as steady help as stable doctrine

*Argue on behalf of your most cherished belief; then argue against it.*

## WEDNESDAY

The female contains all qualities and tempers them,
She is in her place and moves with perfect balance,
She is all things duly veil'd, she is both passive and active

Write what you like and dislike about your mother. Does she "contain all qualities and temper them?"

## THURSDAY

O for the swiftness and balance of fishes!

Write a haiku about balance. A haiku is 3 lines containing 5, 7, and 5 syllables each.

## FRIDAY

O but it is not the years—it is I, it is You,

We touch all laws and tally all antecedents,

We are the skald, the oracle, the monk and the knight, we
easily include them and more,

We stand amid time beginningless and endless, we stand amid
evil and good,

All swings around us, there is as much darkness as light,

The very sun swings itself and its system of planets around us,

Its sun, and its again, all swing around us.

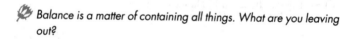 *Balance is a matter of containing all things. What are you leaving out?*

## SATURDAY

The smallest sprout shows there is really no death,

And if ever there was it led forward life, and does not wait at
the end to arrest it,

And ceas'd the moment life appear'd.

All goes onward and outward, nothing collapses,

And to die is different from what any one supposed, and luckier.

What did you inherit from your father's personality? Can you trace it back to his father? Your great-grandfather? Have you embraced or rejected those traits, and how do you bring yourself back to balance regarding them?

## SUNDAY

When I started this week, I knew I was out of balance with the foods I eat and with exercise. I spent much of the week focusing on adding more vegetables into my diet and getting more exercise. Spirit, body and mind felt much more in balance as the week progressed. I also had a great talk with my father as I learned to embrace my inherited traits from his side of our family. Small children and animals have always been attracted to me and I've noticed this about him and remember it about his dad. I'm not sure how it works, but I know it comes from his side of the family. —iKE

## WEEK 24

# HEALTH

## MONDAY

I, now thirty-seven years old in perfect health begin,
Hoping to cease not till death.

*Back to the basics—how is your health? Do you have a balanced approach to nutrition and exercise—not too obsessive, not too slack? What do you need to change? Make a list of 5 things you need to do to improve your health.*

## TUESDAY

Shine! shine! shine!
Pour down your warmth, great sun!
While we bask, we two together.

*Do the first thing on your list. Continue as long as necessary.*

## WEDNESDAY

This face of a healthy honest boy is the programme of all good.

*Do the second thing on your list. Continue as long as necessary.*

## THURSDAY

Women and men in wisdom innocence and health—all joy!

*Do the third thing on your list. Continue as long as necessary.*

## FRIDAY

Thanks in old age—thanks ere I go,
For health, the midday sun, the impalpable air—for life,
    mere life.

*You know how your body feels when you are really in touch with the love you feel for another? It's a physical sensation in your chest. Can you feel that for yourself?*

# SATURDAY

To formulate a poem whose every thought or fact should
directly or indirectly be or connive at an implicit belief in
the wisdom, health, mystery, beauty of every process, every
concrete object, every human or other existence, not only
consider'd from the point of view of all, but of each.

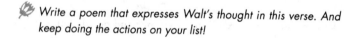 *Write a poem that expresses Walt's thought in this verse. And
keep doing the actions on your list!*

# SUNDAY

*The first thing on my list is to walk for half an hour each day. I sometimes don't manage it—other things get in the way—but I take the long view and don't let the rhythms of life discourage me. Exercise has always been important to me, so I know I'll get back to it. —Connie*

## WEEK 25

# MIND

## MONDAY

O take my hand Walt Whitman!
Such gliding wonders! such sights and sounds!
Such join'd unended links, each hook'd to the next,
Each answering all, each sharing the earth with all.

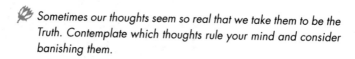 *Take Walt's hand, and tuning into his essential Waltness, draw a picture of him. Don't be concerned about realism. Be expressive.*

## TUESDAY

A prophecy and indirection, a thought impalpable to breathe
as air,

*Sometimes our thoughts seem so real that we take them to be the Truth. Contemplate which thoughts rule your mind and consider banishing them.*

## WEDNESDAY

The sign is reversing, the orb is enclosed,

The ring is circled, the journey is done,

The box-lid is but perceptibly open'd, nevertheless the perfume

pours copiously out of the whole box.

 *Open your mind to the infinite wisdom to be found in the most mundane encounters.*

## THURSDAY

Up from the mystic play of shadows twining and twisting as if

they were alive,

Out from the patches of briers and blackberries,

From the memories of the bird that chanted to me

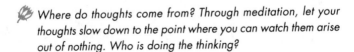 *Where do thoughts come from? Through meditation, let your thoughts slow down to the point where you can watch them arise out of nothing. Who is doing the thinking?*

# FRIDAY

I will make the true poem of riches,
To earn for the body and the mind whatever adheres and goes
forward and is not dropt by death.

*The mind is a wonderful instrument for analysis; there is beauty to be found in its workings. Does your mind carry riches that you have not yet discovered?*

# SATURDAY

How clear is my mind—how all people draw nigh to me!

*Clarity is to be found in the union of mind, body, and spirit, when nothing obstructs the life force. This is a means for living a life. Start now.*

# SUNDAY

*Often, people confuse the mind and the ego. I think of the ego as a virus in the mind. My mind is much like a CPU in a computer. Without it, the computer called iKE cannot play the game of life. I spent this week doing the exercises and noticing how the virus attempted to sabotage the mind's ability to simply process "what is." Often, I simply thank the ego for creating countless opportunities to allow me to choose peace over drama and responsibility over victimhood. –iKE*

# BODY/TOUCH

## MONDAY

Behold, the body includes and is the meaning, the main
concern, and includes and is the soul;
Whoever you are, how superb and how divine is your body, or
any part of it!

 *Can you see your body as divine? If not, what would it take to do so?*

## TUESDAY

I will make the poems of materials, for I think they are to be
the most spiritual poems,
And I will make the poems of my body and of mortality,
For I think I shall then supply myself with the poems of my
soul and of immortality.

 *What do you want done with your body after you die? Why?*

## WEDNESDAY

Such verses for my Body let us write

One's-Self I sing, a simple separate person

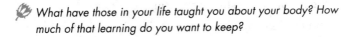 *You are both finite and infinite, mortal and immortal—a supreme paradox. Experiment with this paradox. Can you extend your feeling, consciousness, awareness outside the confines of your body? Or, if that's easy for you, can you be grounded all day?*

## THURSDAY

Here to put your lips upon mine I permit you,

With the comrade's long-dwelling kiss or the new husband's
kiss,

For I am the new husband and I am the comrade.

*What have those in your life taught you about your body? How much of that learning do you want to keep?*

# FRIDAY

The real life of my senses and flesh transcending my senses
and flesh,
My body done with materials, my sight done with my material
eyes,
Proved to me this day beyond cavil that it is not my material
eyes which finally see,
Nor my material body which finally loves, walks, laughs,
shouts, embraces, procreates.

 *Allow inspiration to drive the vehicle of your body throughout this
day.*

# SATURDAY

Of physiology from top to toe I sing,
Not physiognomy alone nor brain alone is worthy for the
Muse, I say the Form complete is worthier far,
The Female equally with the Male I sing.

 *If you are a man, give your feminine side the upper hand. If you're
a woman, let your masculinity shine.*

# SUNDAY

*"The body includes and is the meaning." Whitman is the poet of the body; he sings the body electric. He is not ashamed—he celebrates it. The philosopher and poet George Santayana called Whitman's poetry "the voice of nature crying in the wilderness of convention." While his frankness shocked many in his time, he just wants us to see our bodies as part of nature, and thus as divine expression. Santayana calls this vision "the widening of your sympathies, your reconciliation with nature." –Connie*

# SHADOW

## MONDAY

Two great hulls motionless on the breast of the darkness,
Our vessel riddled and slowly sinking

*What sinks your vessel? When you are deep in the shadows of
your life, what do you see? Write a page or two about it.*

## TUESDAY

Whom have you slaughter'd lately European headsman?
Whose is that blood upon you so wet and sticky?

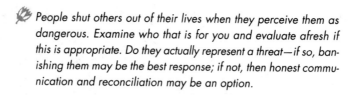

*People shut others out of their lives when they perceive them as
dangerous. Examine who that is for you and evaluate afresh if
this is appropriate. Do they actually represent a threat—if so, banishing them may be the best response; if not, then honest communication and reconciliation may be an option.*

# WEDNESDAY

That is the fluttering, the fluttering of the spray,
Those are the shadows of leaves.
O darkness! O in vain!
O I am very sick and sorrowful.

 *What is the most difficult time you've ever lived through? What pulled you through?*

# THURSDAY

Still here I carry my old delicious burdens,
I carry them, men and women, I carry them with me wherever
   I go,
I swear it is impossible for me to get rid of them,
I am fill'd with them, and I will fill them in return.

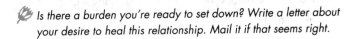 *Is there a burden you're ready to set down? Write a letter about your desire to heal this relationship. Mail it if that seems right.*

# FRIDAY

Who are you? and what are you secretly guilty of all your life?
Will you turn aside all your life? will you grub and chatter all
    your life?

*This is the moment to stop turning aside from who you are.*

# SATURDAY

Demon or bird! (said the boy's soul,)
Is it indeed toward your mate you sing? or is it really to me?
For I, that was a child, my tongue's use sleeping, now I have
    heard you,
Now in a moment I know what I am for, I awake,
And already a thousand singers, a thousand songs, clearer,
    louder and more sorrowful than yours,
A thousand warbling echoes have started to life within me,
    never to die.

*If you completely engaged the purpose of this week, then set this
book down now. You're home free.*

# SUNDAY

*During my divorce, I committed to being 100% responsible for everything I experienced, no matter what happened. As massive challenges came my way, I kept looking at how I was creating this and not anyone or anything outside me. The deeper I held to this idea, the more the very illusion of iKE ALLEN as a person crumbled. As the end of the divorce proceedings arrived, I emerged as Truth. Truth that exists beyond any language or explanation. I still play the game of human being, but I know it's only a game, a game I greatly enjoy. —iKE*

**WEEK 28**

# PRACTICALITY

## MONDAY

Mightier than Egypt's tombs,
Fairer than Grecia's, Roma's temples,
Prouder than Milan's statued, spired cathedral,
More picturesque than Rhenish castle-keeps,
We plan even now to raise, beyond them all,
Thy great cathedral sacred industry, no tomb,
A keep for life for practical invention.

 *Now that you've tasted enlightenment, what do you do with the rest of your life?*

## TUESDAY

The machinist rolls up his sleeves, the policeman travels his
    beat, the gate-keeper marks who pass

*Are you engaging your life as fully as possible? What changes might be required to do so? If you're a machinist, and you can't be the best machinist ever, then what do you do? Play your role as though your life depended on it—it does!*

# WEDNESDAY

Seasons pursuing each other the plougher ploughs, the mower
  mows, and the winter-grain falls in the ground;
Off on the lakes the pike-fisher watches and waits by the hole
  in the frozen surface,
The stumps stand thick round the clearing, the squatter strikes
  deep with his axe,
Flatboatmen make fast towards dusk near the cotton-wood or
  pecan-trees

*If the practical elements of your life aren't attended to, they can suck up a lot of energy you could be spending in more fulfilling ways. Make time to put your house in order.*

# THURSDAY

This is the geologist, this works with the scalpel, and this is a
   mathematician.
Gentlemen, to you the first honors always!
Your facts are useful, and yet they are not my dwelling,
I but enter by them to an area of my dwelling.

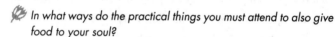 In what ways do the practical things you must attend to also give
food to your soul?

# FRIDAY

Here shall you trace in flowing operation,
In every state of practical, busy movement, the rills of
   civilization

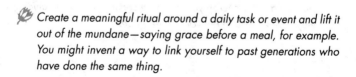 Create a meaningful ritual around a daily task or event and lift it
out of the mundane—saying grace before a meal, for example.
You might invent a way to link yourself to past generations who
have done the same thing.

## SATURDAY

I say I bring thee Muse to-day and here,

All occupations, duties broad and close,

Toil, healthy toil and sweat, endless, without cessation,

The old, old practical burdens, interests, joys

*Find a new and creative way to do everything you do today!*

## SUNDAY

*For Whitman, nothing was quotidian. George Santayana again, taking on Whitman's critics: "...what makes you think the essence poetry distils can't be extracted from every object? Why should one thing leave its type in the world of ideas, and not another! Trust me, beauty is everywhere, if we only had the genius to see it." WW certainly had the genius, and when under his spell I am struck by the mysterious wonders that surround me in ordinary objects (how does a telephone actually work?) and sense the link to untold generations who have performed the same daily tasks (washing the dishes, growing a garden). –Connie*

## WEEK 29

# INTUITION

## MONDAY

You road I enter upon and look around, I believe you are not
    all that is here,
I believe that much unseen is also here.

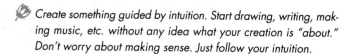 *Create something guided by intuition. Start drawing, writing, making music, etc. without any idea what your creation is "about." Don't worry about making sense. Just follow your intuition.*

## TUESDAY

The workmanship of souls is by those inaudible words of the
    earth,
The masters know the earth's words and use them more than
    audible words.

*Before making any decision, no matter how small, consult your inner voices for guidance. Don't do anything merely by rote.*

## WEDNESDAY

Space and Time! now I see it is true, what I guess'd at,

What I guess'd when I loaf'd on the grass,

What I guess'd while I lay alone in my bed,

And again as I walk'd the beach under the paling stars of the
morning.

My ties and ballasts leave me, my elbows rest in sea-gaps,

I skirt sierras, my palms cover continents,

I am afoot with my vision.

*Walk out your door, and allow intuition to guide your footsteps. Keep your mind as receptive as you can. Sometimes the mere act of moving your feet can shake creative solutions free.*

## THURSDAY

I fly those flights of a fluid and swallowing soul,

My course runs below the soundings of plummets.

I help myself to material and immaterial,

No guard can shut me off, no law prevent me.

*The voice we're calling **intuition** is a message from totality. What other words describe this for you? Make a list and then throw it away.*

........................................................................

## FRIDAY

MEDIUMS

They shall arise in the States,

They shall report Nature, laws, physiology, and happiness,

They shall illustrate Democracy and the kosmos...

Death, the future, the invisible faith, shall all be convey'd.

*We've all had the experience of "reading" someone's mind or having a premonition. If psychic ability is commonplace, then what does that say about our separation from one another? Is this a useful insight?*

........................................................................

## SATURDAY

O soul, repressless, I with thee and thou with me,

Thy circumnavigation of the world begin,

Of man, the voyage of his mind's return,

To reason's early paradise,

Back, back to wisdom's birth, to innocent intuitions,

Again with fair creation.

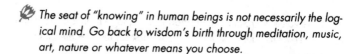

*The seat of "knowing" in human beings is not necessarily the logical mind. Go back to wisdom's birth through meditation, music, art, nature or whatever means you choose.*

# SUNDAY

*Intuition/Inspiration/Passion/God/Maia/The Universe/The Zero Point Field/V. Many names and one destination. It's not just the destination, it's where we all arrived from. As each of the moments of my life operate from this place instead of from the mind, joy fills my being. I continuously live deeper into this place and from there, life is good. —iKE*

## WEEK 30

# CREATIVITY

## MONDAY

O slender leaves! O blossoms of my blood! I permit you to tell
in your own way of the heart that is under you

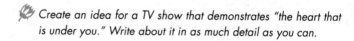 *Create an idea for a TV show that demonstrates "the heart that is under you." Write about it in as much detail as you can.*

## TUESDAY

After all not to create only, or found only,
But to bring perhaps from afar what is already founded,
To give it our own identity, average, limitless, free

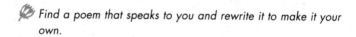 *Find a poem that speaks to you and rewrite it to make it your own.*

# WEDNESDAY

The yellow half-moon enlarged, sagging down, drooping, the
    face of the sea almost touching,

The boy ecstatic, with his bare feet the waves, with his hair the
    atmosphere dallying,

The love in the heart long pent, now loose, now at last
    tumultuously bursting,

The aria's meaning, the ears, the soul, swiftly depositing,

The strange tears down the cheeks coursing,

The colloquy there, the trio, each uttering,

The undertone, the savage old mother incessantly crying,

To the boy's soul's questions sullenly timing, some drown'd
    secret hissing,

To the outsetting bard.

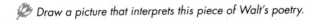 Draw a picture that interprets this piece of Walt's poetry.

# THURSDAY

Dazzling and tremendous how quick the sun-rise would kill me,
If I could not now and always send sun-rise out of me.
We also ascend dazzling and tremendous as the sun,
We found our own O my soul in the calm and cool of the day-break.
My voice goes after what my eyes cannot reach,
With the twirl of my tongue I encompass worlds and volumes
   of worlds.

*Tell someone about something unseen that has touched and inspired you.*

# FRIDAY

Now I will do nothing but listen,
To accrue what I hear into this song, to let sounds contribute
   toward it.
I hear bravuras of birds, bustle of growing wheat, gossip of
   flames, clack of sticks cooking my meals

*Spend your day listening intently and then create a collage that visually expresses what you heard.*

## SATURDAY

That you are here—that life exists and identity,
That the powerful play goes on, and you may contribute a
 verse.

Create something in nature that could be gone a minute or a day later. (For inspiration, Google "Andy Goldsworthy.")

## SUNDAY

I dreamed up a reality show in which the participants get to accomplish a creative goal that they haven't yet found the resources for: paint for a month, write a novel, start a foundation, record a CD of their songs... The show provides them money and time to complete their work, and then they let the world see the results. It's the reality show called **Life**, isn't it? The resources we need to be creative are there. –Connie

## WEEK 31

# CHAOS

## MONDAY

Throb, baffled and curious brain! throw out questions and
 answers!
Suspend here and everywhere, eternal float of solution!

 *Make a list of things you know you don't know.*

## TUESDAY

The way is suspicious, the result uncertain, perhaps destructive,
You would have to give up all else, I alone would expect to be
 your sole and exclusive standard,
Your novitiate would even then be long and exhausting,
The whole past theory of your life and all conformity to the
 lives around you would have to be abandon'd

 *Make a list of things you **don't know** that you don't know.*

## WEDNESDAY

Not in sighs at night in rage dissatisfied with myself,

Not in those long-drawn, ill-supprest sighs,

Not in many an oath and promise broken,

Not in my wilful and savage soul's volition,

Not in the subtle nourishment of the air

*What can you actually prove is true? Can you think of something that everyone agrees is true?*

## THURSDAY

My brain feels rack'd, bewilder'd,

Let the old timbers part, I will not part,

I will cling fast to Thee, O God, though the waves buffet me,

Thee, Thee at least I know.

*Write a letter to God, or whatever you came up with yesterday as truth, and express your perception of God or truth.*

## FRIDAY

What is your money-making now? what can it do now?

What is your respectability now?

What are your theology, tuition, society, traditions, statute-
    books, now?

Where are your jibes of being now?

Where are your cavils about the soul now?

 *Chaos can seem destructive and disorienting, but only if you're
clinging to solutions. Find the wild freedom in letting go in the
midst of chaos.*

## SATURDAY

I permit to speak at every hazard,

Nature without check with original energy.

 *Let your speech be that of original energy. Don't be concerned
about the reactions of others.*

# SUNDAY

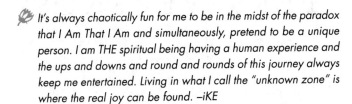 It's always chaotically fun for me to be in the midst of the paradox that I Am That I Am and simultaneously, pretend to be a unique person. I am THE spiritual being having a human experience and the ups and downs and round and rounds of this journey always keep me entertained. Living in what I call the "unknown zone" is where the real joy can be found. —iKE

# PERSEVERENCE

## MONDAY

What do you think endures?

Do you think a great city endures?

Or a teeming manufacturing state? or a prepared constitution? or the best built steamships?

Or hotels of granite and iron? or any chef-d'oeuvres of engineering, forts, armaments?

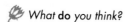 *What **do** you think?*

## TUESDAY

But soft! sink low!

Soft! let me just murmur,

And do you wait a moment you husky-nois'd sea,

For somewhere I believe I heard my mate responding to me,

So faint, I must be still, be still to listen,

But not altogether still, for then she might not come
    immediately to me.

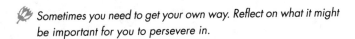 *Persistence requires both the waiting and the urgency to complete your mission. Write out an action plan for an important goal, giving yourself both the latitude and the challenge you need to actually accomplish it.*

## WEDNESDAY

Let me have my own way,
Let others promulge the laws, I will make no account of the laws,
Let others praise eminent men and hold up peace, I hold up
    agitation and conflict,
I praise no eminent man, I rebuke to his face the one that was
    thought most worthy.

*Sometimes you need to get your own way. Reflect on what it might be important for you to persevere in.*

# THURSDAY

I must follow up these continual lessons of the air, water, earth,
I perceive I have no time to lose.

 *Embody both patience and persistence in your endeavors.*

# FRIDAY

Utter defeat upon me weighs—all lost—the foe victorious,
(Yet 'mid the ruins Pride colossal stands unshaken to the last,
Endurance, resolution to the last.)

 *Take a look at the action plan you created on Tuesday. Are you
persisting? If not, why not?*

## SATURDAY

I throw myself upon your breast my father,
I cling to you so that you cannot unloose me,
I hold you so firm till you answer me something.

*Is there unfinished business that you need to clear up with someone in your life? Today is the day to take that on.*

## SUNDAY

*I find that when I balance passion with patience, my efforts tend to bear more fruit. Too much patience yields passivity—nothing gets done; too much passion yields frustration in the face of obstacles, and then I don't have the space to find a creative way around them. —Connie*

## WEEK 33

# LAUGHTER

## MONDAY

I will effuse egotism and show it underlying all, and I will be
the bard of personality

 *Wisdom isn't bland. You don't have to suppress your personality
to live an enlightened life. Loosen up!*

## TUESDAY

With laugh and many a kiss,
(Let others deprecate, let others weep for sin, remorse,
humiliation,)
O soul thou pleasest me, I thee.

 *Tell as many jokes as you can. If you need material, go to
jokes.com.*

## WEDNESDAY

There by the furnace, and there by the anvil,
Behold thy sturdy blacksmiths swinging their sledges,
Overhand so steady, overhand they turn and fall with joyous clank,
Like a tumult of laughter.

 *Find humor in unusual places—your job, the dentist's office, your bills, a phone call with your mother-in-law. Don't stifle the giggles.*

## THURSDAY

O baffled, balk'd, bent to the very earth,
Oppress'd with myself that I have dared to open my mouth,
Aware now that amid all that blab whose echoes recoil upon
    me I have not once had the least idea who or what I am,
But that before all my arrogant poems the real Me stands yet
    untouch'd, untold, altogether unreach'd,
Withdrawn far, mocking me with mock-congratulatory signs
    and bows
With peals of distant ironical laughter at every word I have written,
Pointing in silence to these songs, and then to the sand beneath.

*The joke is on you, and nothing lasts forever. Are you laughing?*

## FRIDAY

…the loud laugh of work-people at their meals

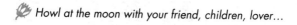 *Have a food fight—we dare you!*

## SATURDAY

I am the ever-laughing—it is new moon and twilight

*Howl at the moon with your friend, children, lover…*

# SUNDAY

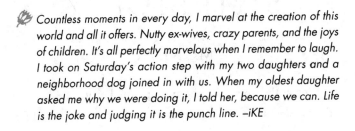

*Countless moments in every day, I marvel at the creation of this world and all it offers. Nutty ex-wives, crazy parents, and the joys of children. It's all perfectly marvelous when I remember to laugh. I took on Saturday's action step with my two daughters and a neighborhood dog joined in with us. When my oldest daughter asked me why we were doing it, I told her, because we can. Life is the joke and judging it is the punch line. –iKE*

## WEEK 34

# SIMPLICITY

## MONDAY

The log at the wood-pile, the axe supported by it,
The sylvan hut, the vine over the doorway, the space clear'd for
a garden,
The irregular tapping of rain down on the leaves after the
storm is lull'd

 *Listen. Really listen.*

## TUESDAY

I see the sleeping babe nestling the breast of its mother,
The sleeping mother and babe—hush'd, I study them long and
long.

 *See.*

## WEDNESDAY

Alone far in the wilds and mountains I hunt,
Wandering amazed at my own lightness and glee,
In the late afternoon choosing a safe spot to pass the night,
Kindling a fire and broiling the fresh-kill'd game,
Falling asleep on the gather'd leaves with my dog and gun by
    my side.

 *Smell.*

## THURSDAY

I perceive I have not really understood any thing, not a single
    object, and that no man ever can,
Nature here in sight of the sea taking advantage of me to dart
    upon me and sting me,
Because I have dared to open my mouth to sing at all.

 *Touch.*

# FRIDAY

I think I could turn and live with animals, they are so placid
    and self-contain'd,

I stand and look at them long and long.

They do not sweat and whine about their condition,

They do not lie awake in the dark and weep for their sins,

They do not make me sick discussing their duty to God,

Not one is dissatisfied, not one is demented with the mania of
    owning things,

Not one kneels to another, nor to his kind that lived thousands
    of years ago,

Not one is respectable or unhappy over the whole earth.

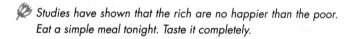 *Studies have shown that the rich are no happier than the poor.
Eat a simple meal tonight. Taste it completely.*

## SATURDAY

Away with old romance!

Away with novels, plots and plays of foreign courts,

Away with love-verses sugar'd in rhyme, the intrigues, amours
  of idlers

*Clean out your closets, your attic, your garage, and dispense with anything that isn't functional or beautiful, or doesn't have meaning for you. Do the same with your mind.*

## SUNDAY

*I'm reasonably good at mind decluttering, but getting rid of the debris that piles up all over my house and office is another matter. I can easily convince myself that I'm going to need that hot water bottle for something, or that I'm sure to travel by bicycle in Southern France someday so let's keep the article about that. But the availability of information on the Internet makes paper info hoarding a bit ridiculous, and the farther I travel in life the more I seem to appreciate simple surroundings. So out it goes—it's satisfying to take boxes of this stuff to Goodwill. –Connie*

# TRANSCENDENCE

## MONDAY

Here spirituality the translatress, the openly-avow'd,
The ever-tending, the finalè of visible forms,
The satisfier, after due long-waiting now advancing,
Yes here comes my mistress the soul.

 *You have an appointment with your soul. What will you wear? Where will you go? What will you say?*

## TUESDAY

Whoever you are! you are he or she for whom the earth is solid
    and liquid,
You are he or she for whom the sun and moon hang in the sky,
For none more than you are the present and the past,
For none more than you is immortality.

*If you do not let yourself be defined by your past, what do you think you might be capable of?*

## WEDNESDAY

For who but I should understand love with all its sorrow and
   joy?

*Love has so many forms, and means different things to different people. If you pare it down to essentials, what is it? Is it about what you like in another, or is it deeper than that?*

## THURSDAY

Bearded, sun-burnt, gray-neck'd, forbidding, I have arrived,
To be wrestled with as I pass for the solid prizes of the
   universe,
For such I afford whoever can persevere to win them.

*What is your biggest obstacle to transcendence? What is your blind spot? Ask your best friend to tell you.*

........................................................................................

# FRIDAY

I am the credulous man of qualities, ages, races,

I advance from the people in their own spirit,

Here is what sings unrestricted faith.

*Reflect on the faith you were raised with, whether that was an organized religion, atheism, humanism, science... Can that faith be a path to transcendence for you?*

........................................................................................

# SATURDAY

Of your real body and any man's or woman's real body,

Item for item it will elude the hands of the corpse-cleaners
    and pass to fitting spheres,

Carrying what has accrued to it from the moment of birth to
    the moment of death.

*Death is the ultimate transcendence. What will die at the moment of your death? What will not?*

# SUNDAY

*To me, trying to transcend yourself is like being a fish in a lake, looking for water. The joke is that you have already transcended and that all you need to do is recognize this. When we peel off the layers of our false identity, our true nature is there, where it always is. You can transcend the egoic mind today, or when you get hit by a bus. The choice is yours. —iKE*

WEEK 36

# FREEDOM

## MONDAY

To the States or any one of them, or any city of the States,
    Resist much, obey little,
Once unquestioning obedience, once fully enslaved,
Once fully enslaved, no nation, state, city of this earth, ever
    afterward resumes its liberty.

 *What keeps you from complete freedom?*

## TUESDAY

Afoot and light-hearted I take to the open road,
Healthy, free, the world before me,
The long brown path before me leading wherever I choose.

 *Go somewhere you've never been.*

## WEDNESDAY

The Originatress comes,
The nest of languages, the bequeather of poems, the race of eld,
Florid with blood, pensive, rapt with musings, hot with passion,
Sultry with perfume, with ample and flowing garments,
With sunburnt visage, with intense soul and glittering eyes,
The race of Brahma comes.

 *Creativity requires freedom from preconceived ideas and old structures. Throw them all away. See what happens. Be free to create.*

## THURSDAY

I call to the world to distrust the accounts of my friends, but
  listen to my enemies, as I myself do,
I charge you forever reject those who would expound me, for I
  cannot expound myself,
I charge that there be no theory or school founded out of me,
I charge you to leave all free, as I have left all free.

 *Could you profit from listening to your "enemies"—to those who may not agree with you?*

# FRIDAY

Thy trills of shrieks by rocks and hills return'd,
Launch'd o'er the prairies wide, across the lakes,
To the free skies unpent and glad and strong.

*Do you associate a particular place with freedom? Perhaps a beautiful spot in nature, or your room—a place where you can do whatever you want? Can you extend that quality to every place you go?*

# SATURDAY

Joy! joy! in freedom, worship, love! joy in the ecstasy of life!
Enough to merely be! enough to breathe!
Joy! joy! all over joy!

*Be free of obligations. Unplug the phone, disconnect the computer. It's your day. Make the most of it.*

# SUNDAY

*The belief that objects, experiences, and other people can make me happy keeps me from freedom. —Connie*

## WEEK 37

# MOVEMENT

### MONDAY

Grow up taller sweet leaves that I may see! grow up out of my
breast!

Spring away from the conceal'd heart there!

Do not fold yourself so in your pink-tinged roots timid leaves!

 *Dance in front of someone even if you think you can't dance. Transcend timidity.*

### TUESDAY

Joys of the solitary walk, the spirit bow'd yet proud

 *Movement and solitude combined often help us sort out challenges. Take a walk, do your workout, run, dance, etc. by yourself, and use this time to dive into the conflicts in your life.*

# WEDNESDAY

We feel the long pulsation, ebb and flow of endless motion,

The tones of unseen mystery, the vague and vast suggestions of
the briny world, the liquid-flowing syllables,

The perfume, the faint creaking of the cordage, the
melancholy rhythm

 *Science tells us that everything is always in motion, at least at an atomic level. Even in places in yourself or your life that you think of as stuck and paralyzed, there are currents of change. See if you can feel the dynamic current in these still places.*

# THURSDAY

Behold, the sea itself,

And on its limitless, heaving breast, the ships;

See, where their white sails, bellying in the wind, speckle the
green and blue,

See, the steamers coming and going, steaming in or out of port,

See, dusky and undulating, the long pennants of smoke.

 *Surround yourself in busyness—go downtown, to a mall, or some-place else full of activity and tune in to the energy uniting you to this locus of motion. Is there stillness within the movement?*

# FRIDAY

Mark the spirit of invention everywhere, thy rapid patents,
Thy continual workshops, foundries, risen or rising,
See, from their chimneys how the tall flame-fires stream.

 *Draw something on a big piece of blank paper without looking at the paper.*

# SATURDAY

O to go back to the place where I was born,
To hear the birds sing once more,
To ramble about the house and barn and over the fields once
    more,
And through the orchard and along the old lanes once more.

 *Think of a place from childhood where you loved to hang out. Get it solidly in your mind—all the details you can remember. Now, in an indoor or outdoor area where you feel comfortable doing this, move around in that remembered space—treat the actual space as the remembered space, and pay attention to how you feel.*

# SUNDAY

*Movement is for most of us one of the most glorious experiences in playing the human game. For the Saturday exercise, I used the vacation spot in Vermont my family went to when I was a child. I "returned" to a favorite wooded stomping ground of my youth and as I walked through remembered forts I'd built 30 years ago, my mind moved with my body in unison, reflecting on all the magical events that had happened there. —iKE*

# VULNERABILITY

## MONDAY

We willing learners of all, teachers of all, and lovers of all.

We have watch'd the seasons dispensing themselves and
passing on,

And have said, Why should not a man or woman do as much
as the seasons, and effuse as much?

 *Choose a trusted partner and let them blindfold you and lead you around the house or yard. Touch things.*

## TUESDAY

The soft voluptuous opiate shades,

The sun just gone, the eager light dispell'd—(I too will soon be
gone, dispell'd,)

A haze—nirwana—rest and night—oblivion.

 *Death is the ultimate vulnerability, and it comes to all. What actions in your life are motivated by the denial of this fact?*

## WEDNESDAY

And a song make I of the One form'd out of all,
The fang'd and glittering One whose head is over all,
Resolute warlike One including and over all,
(However high the head of any else that head is over all.)

 *Write 5 jokes about death.*

## THURSDAY

Me wherever my life is lived, O to be self-balanced for
    contingencies,
To confront night, storms, hunger, ridicule, accidents, rebuffs,
    as the trees and animals do.

 *Sometimes vulnerability is seen as weakness, but the tree that can
bend in the storm will prevail over the one that breaks.*

## FRIDAY

I do not know what you are for, (I do not know what I am for
    myself, nor what any thing is for,)
But I will search carefully for it even in being foil'd,
In defeat, poverty, misconception, imprisonment—for they too
    are great.

*You must be vulnerable to plunge into the mystery of existence.
What clues to direction within the mystery can you detect? What
does life want from you?*

## SATURDAY

O to sail to sea in a ship!
To leave this steady unendurable land,
To leave the tiresome sameness of the streets, the sidewalks
    and the houses,
To leave you O you solid motionless land, and entering a ship,
To sail and sail and sail!

*Go somewhere enthralling, enticing, exciting! Be open to all
adventures that may occur.*

# SUNDAY

*Joke #3: The world goes right on without you when you're gone.*
*—Connie*

## WEEK 39

# DEVOTION

## MONDAY

Who is he that would become my follower?
Who would sign himself a candidate for my affections?

 *Do you feel that you're learning from WW's wisdom? Would you consider yourself devoted to his insight? Why or why not?*

## TUESDAY

The earth does not argue,
Is not pathetic, has no arrangements,
Does not scream, haste, persuade, threaten, promise,
Makes no discriminations, has no conceivable failures,
Closes nothing, refuses nothing, shuts none out

 *Devotion can be a path of surrender and transcendence. In that spirit, devote yourself to serving someone whom you may not necessarily be drawn to. Be kind.*

## WEDNESDAY

I swear the earth shall surely be complete to him or her who
    shall be complete,
The earth remains jagged and broken only to him or her who
    remains jagged and broken.

*"Be the change you want to see"—as with many clichés, there is truth in this. What do you yearn for in the world around you that you have not yet found for yourself? Peace? Love? Charity?*

## THURSDAY

O the joy of my soul leaning pois'd on itself, receiving identity
    through materials and loving them, observing characters
    and absorbing them,
My soul vibrated back to me from them, from sight, hearing,
    touch, reason, articulation, comparison, memory, and the
    like

*Make as deep a connection with each person you encounter as you possibly can.*

## FRIDAY

Thou knowest how before I commenced I devoted all to come
to Thee,

Thou knowest I have in age ratified all those vows and strictly
kept them,

Thou knowest I have not once lost nor faith nor ecstasy in
Thee.

 *What are you most committed to?*

## SATURDAY

The Continent, devoting the whole identity without reserving
an atom,

Pour in! whelm that which asks, which sings, with all and the
yield of all

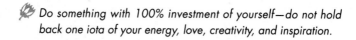 *Do something with 100% investment of yourself—do not hold
back one iota of your energy, love, creativity, and inspiration.*

# SUNDAY

*This week I particularly embraced Tuesday's action step. I looked at people I'd prefer not to deal with and checked in with as many as possible to see if I could assist them with anything or simply chat for a bit. I focused on surrendering all judgment and just being with these people. By devoting myself to surrender, I was generally able to see beyond the challenges these people reflected back at me and simply accept them, and me, for all that we are.*
*—iKE*

## WEEK 40

# RESPONSIBILITY

## MONDAY

O while I live to be the ruler of life, not a slave,
To meet life as a powerful conqueror,
No fumes, no ennui, no more complaints or scornful
    criticisms,
To these proud laws of the air, the water and the ground,
    proving my interior soul impregnable,
And nothing exterior shall ever take command of me.

 *Your first and most important responsibility is to yourself.*

## TUESDAY

I take part, I see and hear the whole

 *Responsibility requires responsiveness to everything in your life. Don't leave anything out.*

## WEDNESDAY

Thither as I look I see each result and glory retracing itself and
    nestling close, always obligated,
Thither hours, months, years—thither trades, compacts,
    establishments, even the most minute,
Thither every-day life, speech, utensils, politics, persons,
    estates;
Thither we also, I with my leaves and songs, trustful, admirant,
As a father to his father going takes his children along with
    him.

*Begin with those already in your life. Is there anything you need to do for them?*

## THURSDAY

Whoever you are! claim your own at any hazard!
These shows of the East and West are tame compared to you,
These immense meadows, these interminable rivers, you are
    immense and interminable as they.

*Many people aren't able to see their reactions to others as their own responsibility. But no one "makes" you angry, which is not to say that their actions may not warrant an angry response. You can't control others' reactions, and they can't control yours.*

## FRIDAY

Aboard at a ship's helm,

A young steersman steering with care.

Through fog on a sea-coast dolefully ringing,

An ocean-bell—O a warning bell, rock'd by the waves.

O you give good notice indeed, you bell by the sea-reefs ringing,

Ringing, ringing, to warn the ship from its wreck-place.

 *Be alert to the gentlest of warning signs and respond appropriately.*

## SATURDAY

I saw old General at bay,

(Old as he was, his gray eyes yet shone out in battle like stars,)

His small force was now completely hemm'd in, in his works,

He call'd for volunteers to run the enemy's lines, a desperate
    emergency,

I saw a hundred and more step forth from the ranks, but two
or three were selected,

I saw them receive their orders aside, they listen'd with care,
the adjutant was very grave,

I saw them depart with cheerfulness, freely risking their lives.

*What would you risk your life for?*

## SUNDAY

*Life has many ways to speak to you. This morning there was a
spider in the shower—I'd observed her in the bathroom for days,
and we had kept our distance. But this morning I wanted her gone
and turned on the shower to wash her down the drain. She scurried
to safety, so I admitted defeat, shut off the water, and returned to
my bedroom to get dressed. When I was ready to leave, there
she was, waiting patiently outside my bedroom door. Was she
imploring or scolding me? What could I do but escort her gently
outside. –Connie*

## WEEK 41

# DOUBT

## MONDAY

Will you rot your own fruit in yourself there?
Will you squat and stifle there?

 *Doubt is often a waste of time (though a very common experience for human beings), especially when it leads to paralysis. That kind of doubt is another name for fear. Shake up your doubts and be free to act on inspiration!*

## TUESDAY

When I undertake to tell the best I find I cannot,
My tongue is ineffectual on its pivots,
My breath will not be obedient to its organs,
I become a dumb man.

 *Is there a particular area of your life in which doubt is pervasive—relationships, work, creativity...? On paper, express the best vision you can imagine for this arena, overriding any doubts that arise as you do so.*

## WEDNESDAY

High and clear I shoot my voice over the waves,

Surely you must know who is here, is here,

You must know who I am, my love.

*Who doubts you? If you let that influence you, why do you?*

## THURSDAY

A word then, (for I will conquer it,)

The word final, superior to all,

Subtle, sent up—what is it?—I listen;

Are you whispering it, and have been all the time, you sea-
waves?

Is that it from your liquid rims and wet sands?

*Write the final word.*

# FRIDAY

O trumpeter, methinks I am myself the instrument thou
    playest,
Thou melt'st my heart, my brain—thou movest, drawest,
    changest them at will;
And now thy sullen notes send darkness through me,
Thou takest away all cheering light, all hope.

 *Are you harboring false hope when a better alignment with reality
would serve you and others better?*

# SATURDAY

Logic and sermons never convince,
The damp of the night drives deeper into my soul.

 *Doubt is a useful tool against dogma. Ask questions whenever
you feel the weight of belief pressing on you. Question authority,
as the bumper sticker would have it.*

# SUNDAY

*I learned years ago that with everything in life, only my own personal direct experience would remove my doubt. Like everything, this isn't totally true as I often do take what others say to be true and at the same time, if I want to know what chocolate ice cream tastes like, it's much easier to give it a lick then ask another to describe it for me. Doubt put in motion leads to trust. —iKE*

## WEEK 42

# INDEPENDENCE

## MONDAY

You are also asking me questions and I hear you,
I answer that I cannot answer, you must find out for yourself.

 *Ignore everything we've said in this book. Find your own truth.*

## TUESDAY

Henceforth I ask not good-fortune, I myself am good-fortune,
Henceforth I whimper no more, postpone no more, need
    nothing,
Done with indoor complaints, libraries, querulous criticisms,
Strong and content I travel the open road.

 *Are you your own good fortune? Or do you depend on others to provide it?*

## WEDNESDAY

What about these likes of myself that draw me so close by
tender directions and indirections?

🌿 *Are you living your life's mission?*

## THURSDAY

I wear my hat as I please indoors or out.

🌿 *Wear whatever you want. Be independent in your choices!*

# FRIDAY

Out of the cradle endlessly rocking,

Out of the mocking-bird's throat, the musical shuttle,

Out of the Ninth-month midnight,

Over the sterile sands and the fields beyond, where the child
    leaving his bed wander'd alone, bareheaded, barefoot

 *What didn't you get to do as a child that you really, really wanted to do?*

# SATURDAY

All night long on the prong of a moss-scallop'd stake,

Down almost amid the slapping waves,

Sat the lone singer wonderful causing tears.

 *What piece of music, art, poetry, etc. moves you to tears? If you can, revisit it.*

# SUNDAY

*We've mixed independence with messages of passion and mission this week because they are linked. Sometimes we must respond to Thoreau's "different drummer" to pursue creative ideas and discover our own meaning. It has been very liberating to understand that what others think of me is not my concern. —Connie*

## WEEK 43

# DUALITY

## MONDAY

Did we think victory great?

So it is—but now it seems to me, when it cannot be help'd,
that defeat is great,

And that death and dismay are great.

 *When have you experienced a defeat that later turned out to be helpful to you? (Loss of a job or relationship, for example.)*

## TUESDAY

Urge and urge and urge,

Always the procreant urge of the world.

 *What is creation for?*

## WEDNESDAY

Strange and hard that paradox true I give,
Objects gross and the unseen soul are one.

 *To paraphrase Einstein, "Duality is an illusion, albeit a very persistent one." Ignore the world of gross objects at your peril. What in this realm needs your attention, and can you attend to it while still understanding the illusion?*

## THURSDAY

The song is to the singer, and comes back most to him,
The teaching is to the teacher, and comes back most to him,
The murder is to the murderer, and comes back most to him,
The theft is to the thief, and comes back most to him,
The love is to the lover, and comes back most to him,
The gift is to the giver, and comes back most to him—it
    cannot fail,
The oration is to the orator, the acting is to the actor and
    actress not to the audience,
And no man understands any greatness or goodness but his
    own, or the indication of his own.

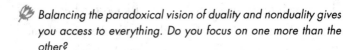 Do you see the law of karma acting in your life? What are your actions creating and are you satisfied with the results? Actions are an investment and they yield a return. Do you need to make new investments?

# FRIDAY

As in a waking vision,

E'en while I chant I see it rise, I scan and prophesy outside
and in,

Its manifold ensemble.

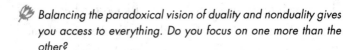 Balancing the paradoxical vision of duality and nonduality gives you access to everything. Do you focus on one more than the other?

## SATURDAY

The city sleeps and the country sleeps,

The living sleep for their time, the dead sleep for their time,

The old husband sleeps by his wife and the young husband
    sleeps by his wife;

And these tend inward to me, and I tend outward to them,

And such as it is to be of these more or less I am,

And of these one and all I weave the song of myself.

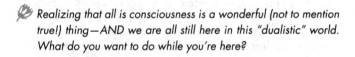 *Realizing that all is consciousness is a wonderful (not to mention true!) thing—AND we are all still here in this "dualistic" world. What do you want to do while you're here?*

## SUNDAY

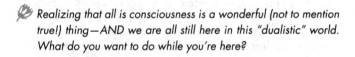 *Oneness and duality are a never ending, simultaneously existing paradox. To be in this world but not of this world is where the real joy is for me. I love pretending to be a father, a lover, a friend. Being the Creator of this world and actually getting to participate in it in many forms, what a dream for me and for you if we recognize it for what it is. Enjoy it all. –iKE*

# NONDUALITY

## MONDAY

I will not make poems with reference to parts,
But I will make poems, songs, thoughts, with reference to
ensemble,
And I will not sing with reference to a day, but with reference
to all days,
And I will not make a poem nor the least part of a poem but
has reference to the soul,
Because having look'd at the objects of the universe, I find
there is no one nor any particle of one but has reference to
the soul.

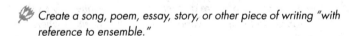 Create a song, poem, essay, story, or other piece of writing "with
reference to ensemble."

# TUESDAY

What widens within you Walt Whitman?

What waves and soils exuding?

What climes? what persons and cities are here?

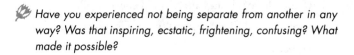 *Whitman liked to refer to himself in the third person. Try that your-self in something you write or say today. What effect does it have on you?*

# WEDNESDAY

None separate from thee—henceforth One only, we and thou

*Have you experienced not being separate from another in any way? Was that inspiring, ecstatic, frightening, confusing? What made it possible?*

## THURSDAY

Whoever you are! motion and reflection are especially for you,
The divine ship sails the divine sea for you.

 *Whatever is going on here, it seems incontrovertible that the divine ship sails the divine sea for you, and for each of us. What other way could it possibly be? And yet we do not trust it. We want solid land, with our own private garden...no slugs or spider mites allowed.*

## FRIDAY

As for me, (torn, stormy, amid these vehement days,)
I have the idea of all, and am all and believe in all,
I believe materialism is true and spiritualism is true, I reject
    no part.

 *In the current climate of spiritual teachings, groups, and gatherings, do you think you would meet resistance if you professed a belief in materialism? What would your life be if it wasn't guided by such divisions—by what you believe in or don't believe in, like or don't like? Will you "reject no part"?*

## SATURDAY

I know that the past was great and the future will be great,
And I know that both curiously conjoint in the present time,
(For the sake of him I typify, for the common average man's
    sake, your sake if you are he,)
And that where I am or you are this present day, there is the
    centre of all days, all races,
And there is the meaning to us of all that has ever come of
    races and days, or ever will come.

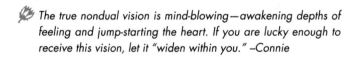

It's not hard to wish you were living a different life. Once I was going through a difficult passage and remarked to a friend that I'd be glad when it was over. "Don't be wishing your life away!" he very wisely said. Choicelessness gives us an appreciation of the "meaning to us of all that has ever come." Have you seen the beauty in the life that is yours?

## SUNDAY

The true nondual vision is mind-blowing—awakening depths of feeling and jump-starting the heart. If you are lucky enough to receive this vision, let it "widen within you." –Connie

# RECEPTIVENESS

## MONDAY

Here the profound lesson of reception, nor preference nor
    denial,

The black with his woolly head, the felon, the diseas'd, the
    illiterate person, are not denied...

They pass, I also pass, any thing passes, none can be
    interdicted,

None but are accepted, none but shall be dear to me.

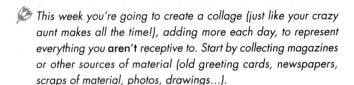 *This week you're going to create a collage (just like your crazy aunt makes all the time!), adding more each day, to represent everything you **aren't** receptive to. Start by collecting magazines or other sources of material (old greeting cards, newspapers, scraps of material, photos, drawings...).*

## TUESDAY

I swear there is no greatness or power that does not emulate
    those of the earth,
There can be no theory of any account unless it corroborate
    the theory of the earth,
No politics, song, religion, behavior, or what not, is of account,
    unless it compare with the amplitude of the earth,
Unless it face the exactness, vitality, impartiality, rectitude of
    the earth.

*Add material to your collage that relates to political, environmental, religious, or social events and ideas that you cannot accept.*

## WEDNESDAY

What is commonest, cheapest, nearest, easiest, is Me,
Me going in for my chances, spending for vast returns,
Adorning myself to bestow myself on the first that will take me,
Not asking the sky to come down to my good will,
Scattering it freely forever.

*What are the things you have trouble accepting in yourself? More fodder for your fantastic collage in the making.*

## THURSDAY

What you give me I cheerfully accept,

A little sustenance, a hut and garden, a little money, as I
rendezvous with my poems,

A traveler's lodging and breakfast as I journey through the States,

—why should I be ashamed to own such gifts? why to
advertise for them?

For I myself am not one who bestows nothing upon man and
woman,

For I bestow upon any man or woman the entrance to all the
gifts of the universe.

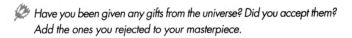 *Have you been given any gifts from the universe? Did you accept them?
Add the ones you rejected to your masterpiece.*

## FRIDAY

I swear I begin to see love with sweeter spasms than that
which responds love,

It is that which contains itself, which never invites and never
refuses.

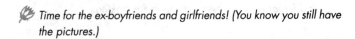 *Time for the ex-boyfriends and girlfriends! (You know you still have
the pictures.)*

## SATURDAY

With the thousand responsive songs at random,

My own songs awaked from that hour,

And with them the key, the word up from the waves,

The word of the sweetest song and all songs,

That strong and delicious word which, creeping to my feet,

(Or like some old crone rocking the cradle, swathed in sweet
garments, bending aside,)

The sea whisper'd me.

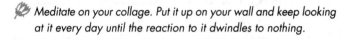

Meditate on your collage. Put it up on your wall and keep looking
at it every day until the reaction to it dwindles to nothing.

## SUNDAY

I still find moments where I'm challenged to receive. I spent the
week noticing my reactions when others wanted to support me
in any manner. Whether it was an offer to get me a cup of coffee
or for a backrub, I noticed my resistance and then accepted the
offers. Many of us want things—are we willing to actually receive
them when they arrive? –iKE

# EIDELONS

## MONDAY

I see the clear sunsets of the martyrs,

I see from the scaffolds the descending ghosts,

Ghosts of dead lords, uncrown'd ladies, impeach'd ministers,
    rejected kings,

Rivals, traitors, poisoners, disgraced chieftains and the rest.

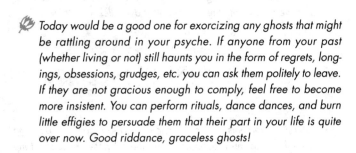 Today would be a good one for exorcizing any ghosts that might be rattling around in your psyche. If anyone from your past (whether living or not) still haunts you in the form of regrets, longings, obsessions, grudges, etc. you can ask them politely to leave. If they are not gracious enough to comply, feel free to become more insistent. You can perform rituals, dance dances, and burn little effigies to persuade them that their part in your life is quite over now. Good riddance, graceless ghosts!

## TUESDAY

I met a seer,

Passing the hues and objects of the world,

The fields of art and learning, pleasure, sense,

To glean eidólons.

*An eidolon is a phantom, an apparition, an ideal. How might our poet be using the word here? Do you think you're like the seer?*

## WEDNESDAY

Not this the world,

Nor these the universes, they the universes,

Purport and end, ever the permanent life of life,

Eidolons, eidolons.

*In Hinduism and Buddhism, maya is the illusion we must see through to be free. The seeming permanence and independence of objects, and the seeming reality of time and space, make up the illusion. But this doesn't make the world a mirage, or unimportant. Merely impermanent, and dependent on consciousness.*

# THURSDAY

The noiseless myriads,

The infinite oceans where the rivers empty,

The separate countless free identities, like eyesight,

The true realities, eidólons.

 *Consider the many millions of people who have lived on earth, and then died, and the many more yet to come—all feeling themselves to be the center of their own existence. And so they were, even though to Life they were dispensable, temporary.*

# FRIDAY

Densities, growth, façades,

Strata of mountains, soils, rocks, giant trees,

Far-born, far-dying, living long, to leave,

Eidólons everlasting.

 *Our lives contain strata—the layers of experiences, thoughts, feelings, and actions through which we have lived, even though much of it is lost to memory. As you reflect on the strata that have produced the unique entity you now are, see if you're inspired to express them through some medium or media. You could use found objects, articles of nature (twigs, leaves, flowers, dirt),*

*papier-mâché, yarn, etc. Create a sculpture of your life.*

## SATURDAY

Of every human life,

(The units gather'd, posted, not a thought, emotion, deed, left
out,)

The whole or large or small summ'd, added up,

In its eidólon.

*If yesterday you did indeed produce a work of art that adds up the layers of your life, does anything about that surprise or inform you? Is there something essential about it? If you were a playwright, what would you title the play of your life?*

## SUNDAY

*One can develop a knack for accepting impermanence without detachment creeping in. And the deeper you go into this, the less you understand it. In the end, you just live. —Connie*

## WEEK 47

# VITALITY

## MONDAY

Leaves from you I glean, I write, to be perused best afterwards,
Tomb-leaves, body-leaves growing up above me above death,
Perennial roots, tall leaves, O the winter shall not freeze you
    delicate leaves,
Every year shall you bloom again, out from where you retired
    you shall emerge again

 *What physical activity did you used to engage in that was incredibly fun, and that you haven't experienced for some time? (Rollerblading, dancing, hiking, basketball, yoga...) It's time to re-engage in this activity.*

## TUESDAY

My respiration and inspiration, the beating of my heart, the
    passing of blood and air through my lungs,
The sniff of green leaves and dry leaves, and of the shore and

dark-color'd sea-rocks, and of hay in the barn

*Tap into the energy in your body—where is it blocked? Do something to increase the energy flow—a massage, deep breathing, running…*

## WEDNESDAY

Murmuring out of its myriad leaves,

Down from its lofty top rising two hundred feet high,

Out of its stalwart trunk and limbs, out of its foot-thick bark,

That chant of the seasons and time, chant not of the past only

but the future.

*Push yourself just a little bit. Don't do anything unsafe please, but find a way to go beyond what you think are your physical limitations, and wake up a little sore tomorrow morning!*

## THURSDAY

Parting track'd by arriving, perpetual payment of perpetual loan,

Rich showering rain, and recompense richer afterward.

Sprouts take and accumulate, stand by the curb prolific and vital,

Landscapes projected masculine, full-sized and golden.

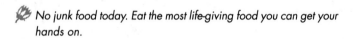 *What are the activities in your life that have the most juice, that are most vital for you?*

---

# FRIDAY

The delight alone or in the rush of the streets, or along the
    fields and hill-sides,
The feeling of health, the full-noon trill, the song of me rising
    from bed and meeting the sun.

*No junk food today. Eat the most life-giving food you can get your hands on.*

---

# SATURDAY

Above all, lo, the sky so calm, so transparent after the rain, and
    with wondrous clouds,
Below too, all calm, all vital and beautiful, and the farm
    prospers well.

*Do something this weekend that unites calmness and vitality.*

# SUNDAY

*I increased my exercise with walks and yoga and ate fresh salads for almost every lunch and dinner this week. By the weekend, I was a bit sore and felt vibrant, alert and light. It's always amazing to me how my body seems to love greens and makes my nose run when I eat dairy. This week has reminded me of the joy of riding my bicycle, even if it's only around a few blocks. –iKE*

# PEACE

## MONDAY

Peace is always beautiful,
The myth of heaven indicates peace and night.

*Think of someone you've struggled with but no longer know how to contact, and write them a letter about your desire for peace.*

## TUESDAY

I loafe and invite my soul,
I lean and loafe at my ease observing a spear of summer grass.

*Do as the poet does, as fully as you can. If a spear of summer grass is nowhere to be had, then plenty of innocent, alive, and humble things can substitute. Leaning, loafing, and inviting at your ease are the indispensable activities of the day.*

## WEDNESDAY

Practical, peaceful life, the people's life, the People themselves,
Lifted, illumin'd, bathed in peace—elate, secure in peace.

*All beings deserve peace. May you be "lifted, illumin'd, bathed" in it.*

## THURSDAY

The best of the earth cannot be told anyhow, all or any is best,
It is not what you anticipated, it is cheaper, easier, nearer,
Things are not dismiss'd from the places they held before,
The earth is just as positive and direct as it was before,
Facts, religions, improvements, politics, trades, are as real as
    before,
But the soul is also real, it too is positive and direct,
No reasoning, no proof has establish'd it,
Undeniable growth has establish'd it.

*You do not need to do anything to change yourself.*

## FRIDAY

Two feather'd guests from Alabama, two together,
And their nest, and four light-green eggs spotted with brown,
And every day the he-bird to and fro near at hand,
And every day the she-bird crouch'd on her nest, silent, with
    bright eyes,
And every day I, a curious boy, never too close, never
    disturbing them,

*The curious boy within gets to witness the miracles of the day and will draw the feather'd guests to him if you let him.*

## SATURDAY

Away with themes of war! away with war itself!
Hence from my shuddering sight to never more return that
    show of blacken'd, mutilated corpses!

*If you're so inspired, help the embattled of the world come closer to peace. Amnesty International has letters for you to write, and your local anti-war group could probably use some assistance.*

## SUNDAY

*More than once I've looked closely at my desire for distraction, excitement, and fulfillment and found that what I truly want is peace. –Connie*

## WEEK 49

# EMPTINESS

## MONDAY

Of the empty and useless years of the rest, with the rest me
    intertwined,
The question, O me! so sad, recurring—What good amid these,
O me, O life?

 *Emptiness can be seen as a lack of something or as potential yet unfulfilled.*

## TUESDAY

The atmosphere is not a perfume, it has no taste of the
    distillation, it is odorless,
It is for my mouth forever, I am in love with it,
I will go to the bank by the wood and become undisguised and
    naked,
I am mad for it to be in contact with me.

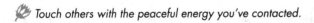 *Do some form of meditation that puts you in touch with the still, overflowing, peaceful energy of emptiness.*

## WEDNESDAY

It alone is without flaw, it alone rounds and completes all,
That mystic baffling wonder alone completes all.

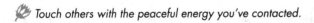 *Create a work of art inspired by your meditation yesterday.*

## THURSDAY

Divine am I inside and out, and I make holy whatever I touch
   or am touch'd from

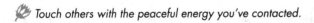 *Touch others with the peaceful energy you've contacted.*

# FRIDAY

Steep'd amid honey'd morphine, my windpipe throttled in
  fakes of death,
At length let up again to feel the puzzle of puzzles,
And that we call Being.

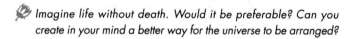 *Imagine life without death. Would it be preferable? Can you create in your mind a better way for the universe to be arranged?*

# SATURDAY

To be in any form, what is that?
(Round and round we go, all of us, and ever come back
  thither)

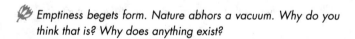 *Emptiness begets form. Nature abhors a vacuum. Why do you think that is? Why does anything exist?*

# SUNDAY

*Buddhism calls God the Void. This has always resonated with me as it seems when I "empty my cup" this allows something magnificent to be poured into it. I live the majority of my human experience from the consciousness of the Void and find it to be much more rewarding. My life unfolds joyously as I keep the ego in the secondary role and allow my true nature to drive my body around the human amusement park. Emptiness is not as empty as many people think.* –iKE

## WEEK 50

# UNDERSTANDING

## MONDAY

Shut not your doors to me proud libraries,
For that which was lacking on all your well-fill'd shelves, yet
    needed most, I bring,
Forth from the war emerging, a book I have made,
The words of my book nothing, the drift of it every thing,
A book separate, not link'd with the rest nor felt by the intellect,
But you ye untold latencies will thrill to every page.

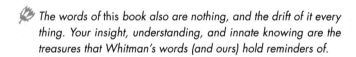 *The words of this book also are nothing, and the drift of it every thing. Your insight, understanding, and innate knowing are the treasures that Whitman's words (and ours) hold reminders of.*

## TUESDAY

They will elude you at first and still more afterward, I will
 certainly elude you,
Even while you should think you had unquestionably caught
 me, behold!
Already you see I have escaped from you.

 *The deepest understanding must be invited in with respect and sincerity. Give it an honored place and your full attention, but don't beg it to stay.*

## WEDNESDAY

Long and long has the grass been growing,
Long and long has the rain been falling,
Long has the globe been rolling round.

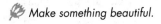 *Make something beautiful.*

## THURSDAY

A song of the rolling earth, and of words according,

Were you thinking that those were the words, those upright lines? those curves, angles, dots?

No, those are not the words, the substantial words are in the ground and sea,

They are in the air, they are in you.

 *Give yourself a good bit of time to sit quietly today, and listen to the substantial words in you.*

## FRIDAY

Air, soil, water, fire—those are words,

I myself am a word with them—my qualities interpenetrate with theirs—my name is nothing to them,

Though it were told in the three thousand languages, what would air, soil, water, fire, know of my name?

 *Invite the understanding beyond words—the understanding of air, soil, water, fire.*

## SATURDAY

With my fathers and mothers and the accumulations of past ages,

With all which, had it not been, I would not now be here, as I am,

🔥 *Think of the people who have loved you without reservation. What have you learned from them? Write about the realizations others have helped you find.*

## SUNDAY

🔥 *What we tell ourselves we believe is not what we live by. We respond to life as we understand it, and our partial understanding can take us in strange and surprising directions. Paying close attention may help understanding grow, but it mostly seems to come as a gift. I hope to stay available for the gift. –Connie*

# HAPPINESS

## MONDAY

Joys of the thought of Death, the great spheres Time and Space?
Prophetic joys of better, loftier love's ideals, the divine wife, the
sweet, eternal, perfect comrade?
Joys all thine own undying one, joys worthy thee O soul.

*Tonight, go to the prettiest place you know with someone you love and hold a picnic under the stars. Bring your own and your companion's favorite foods. If the weather isn't suitable for being outdoors, picnic indoors in a place that makes you happy.*

## TUESDAY

O to have life henceforth a poem of new joys!
To dance, clap hands, exult, shout, skip, leap, roll on, float on!
To be a sailor of the world bound for all ports,
A ship itself, (see indeed these sails I spread to the sun and air,)
A swift and swelling ship full of rich words, full of joys.

*✍ Write the happiest poem on earth.*

---

# WEDNESDAY

Each moment and whatever happens thrills me with joy,
I cannot tell how my ankles bend, nor whence the cause of my
   faintest wish,
Nor the cause of the friendship I emit, nor the cause of the
   friendship I take again.

*✍ Pray to whatever gods you hold dear to let you be happy for no
reason!*

---

# THURSDAY

Mine is no callous shell,
I have instant conductors all over me whether I pass or stop,
They seize every object and lead it harmlessly through me.
I merely stir, press, feel with my fingers, and am happy

*✍ Experience the happiness of touch.*

# FRIDAY

I believe a leaf of grass is no less than the journey-work of the
  stars,

And the pismire is equally perfect, and a grain of sand, and the
  egg of the wren,

And the tree-toad is a chef-d'oeuvre for the highest,

And the running blackberry would adorn the parlors of
  heaven,

And the narrowest hinge in my hand puts to scorn all
  machinery,

And the cow crunching with depress'd head surpasses any
  statue,

And a mouse is miracle enough to stagger sextillions of
  infidels.

*Make a miracle happen—give it every ounce of your creativity,
love, and passion.*

# SATURDAY

O glad, exulting, culminating song!

A vigor more than earth's is in thy notes,

Marches of victory—man disenthral'd—the conqueror at last,

Hymns to the universal God from universal man—all joy!

A reborn race appears—a perfect world, all joy!

 *Say yes to life.*

# SUNDAY

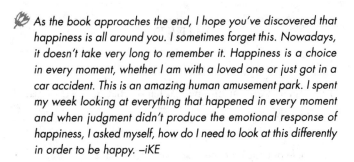 *As the book approaches the end, I hope you've discovered that happiness is all around you. I sometimes forget this. Nowadays, it doesn't take very long to remember it. Happiness is a choice in every moment, whether I am with a loved one or just got in a car accident. This is an amazing human amusement park. I spent my week looking at everything that happened in every moment and when judgment didn't produce the emotional response of happiness, I asked myself, how do I need to look at this differently in order to be happy. –iKE*

# CELEBRATION

## MONDAY

I celebrate myself, and sing myself,

And what I assume you shall assume,

For every atom belonging to me as good belongs to you.

 *Connect with someone you haven't communicated with for a while and re-establish your friendship.*

## TUESDAY

I have seen the he-bird also,

I have paus'd to hear him near at hand inflating his throat and
    joyfully singing.

 *Smile at people on the street. Really BIG smiles.*

## WEDNESDAY

This then is life,

Here is what has come to the surface after so many throes and
convulsions.

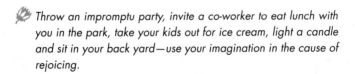 *And this is your life—your one and only astounding, essential,
absurd, resplendent, serious, wide, heartbreaking, full life! May
you find many ways to celebrate, and draw others into the bless-
ings of it.*

## THURSDAY

Good or bad I never question you—I love all—I do not
condemn any thing,

I chant and celebrate all that is yours

*Throw an impromptu party, invite a co-worker to eat lunch with
you in the park, take your kids out for ice cream, light a candle
and sit in your back yard—use your imagination in the cause of
rejoicing.*

## FRIDAY

Onward we move, a gay gang of blackguards! with mirth-
    shouting
 music and wild-flapping pennants of joy!

🌺 *Use music to delight in the day—make some, listen to some, give some.*

## SATURDAY

O amazement of things—even the least particle!
O spirituality of things!

🌺 *Treat yourself well. Treat all of creation well. Even the least particle.*

# SUNDAY

*You've made it through the book, the year, another part of your unique, irreplaceable life. Whitman has had many things to say to you—wisdom that can carry you into the unknown, the miracles yet to come. We wish you every happiness, and the deep joy of understanding. Thanks for making the trip with us! —Connie and iKE*

PHOTO: JOSHUA EDWARDS

PHOTO: www.christinagressianu.com

# ABOUT THE AUTHORS

Connie Shaw is the publisher at Sentient Publications, which focuses on books with fresh perspectives on holistic health, transformative spirituality, alternative education, and ecology. She is a lifelong explorer of poetry, and that, combined with her taste for the quixotic search for truth, kindled her interest in creating this book with Ike. She lives in Boulder, Colorado.

Ike Allen is the founder of AVAIYA, www.avaiya.com. AVAIYA creates transformative movies, such as *Leap!*, *A Course In Miracles: The Movie*, and *MPower: Empowering Women in Business and Beyond.*

Ike used to play a game called Ask Walt with his buddy A.J., in which Whitman's poetry served as an oracle for their questions. His fond memories of that experience generated the idea for this book.

Ike's ultimate passion is experiencing the joys and challenges of raising two gorgeous daughters to live a life of true power, fun and exploration. He lives in Boulder, Colorado.

Both authors can be contacted through their website, dailytao.net, where you can also interact with other readers of this book.

Sentient Publications, LLC publishes books on cultural creativity, experimental education, transformative spirituality, holistic health, new science, ecology, and other topics, approached from an integral viewpoint. Our authors are intensely interested in exploring the nature of life from fresh perspectives, addressing life's great questions, and fostering the full expression of the human potential. Sentient Publications' books arise from the spirit of inquiry and the richness of the inherent dialogue between writer and reader.

Our Culture Tools series is designed to give social catalyzers and cultural entrepreneurs the essential information, technology, and inspiration to forge a sustainable, creative, and compassionate world.

We are very interested in hearing from our readers. To direct suggestions or comments to us, or to be added to our mailing list, please contact:

## SENTIENT PUBLICATIONS, LLC

1113 Spruce Street
Boulder, CO 80302
303-443-2188
contact@sentientpublications.com
www.sentientpublications.com